Are You
Wonderful?

Good Science Says, Yes

HOW TO TELL GOOD SCIENCE FROM BAD

By Shaun Johnston

EVOLVED
SELF
PUBLISHING

Are You Wonderful? Good Science Says, Yes.
How to tell good science from bad
By Shaun Johnston

Published by
Evolved Self Publishing
evolvedself.com
shaunj@evolvedself.com

Table of Contents

Are you wonderful? This book says, yes.

It shows you how wonderful you already are.

In 40 steps, in eight sections, it offers you a path to becoming even more wonderful, through discovering new meaning in life.

The 40 steps are best read in order.

But if you're the kind of reader who goes straight to a book's "Conclusion" to see if it's likely to interest you, head to the final Step, "Spoiler."

STEP 1
Meaning in life

Are you wonderful? Not just, do other people think you're wonderful but do you feel wonderful, inside? Do you feel as wonderful as you could? What could help you feel more wonderful?

Let's call that "meaning in life." Then the more meaning in life you have, the more wonderful you'll feel. You just need to know where to find that kind of meaning.

I think I can help you.

I'm a cut and dried, rational kind of guy, I'm not what you'd call "spiritual." Usually I look to science for answers. But when it comes to meaning in life, science can come with meanings attached to it that lead us astray. I think that's happening today. I think today's science sometimes comes with a meaning that casts a dark shadow over us, over how we think about ourselves, over what life means.

When science comes with meaning attached to it like that, then it's no longer about just facts. It becomes a magic. Astrology grew like that, out of ancient astronomy. Alchemy grew out of experience working with metals. At first a magic like that seems to tell us what the science really means. But then we can apply it to tell us what something else means, like life itself.

This book will help you tell the good meanings science comes with from the bad.

When you're faced with a magic that could harm you, a dark magic, how should you defend yourself? With logic? In my experience, logic doesn't work against magics. Religion? Perhaps at some other time, but not here, today, not for me anyway. In the end I said to myself, the only way to deal with a dark magic that could harm you is to come up with another magic to take its place. That's what I decided to do. I've a magical side—besides being a science writer I'm also a novelist, an artist and an inventor. To counter science's dark magic I set myself to look in science for a new white magic.

I took facts from a particular branch of modern science and came up with a theory about them I could use to give our own lives more meaning. I settled on today's most revolutionary science, modern biology. I took what I knew about genetics and evolution and came up with a new theory to account for them.

I think the magic I came up with could help you find new meaning in life and feel more wonderful. Let me tell you about it.

Four foundational principles

In this first Section
I lay out four principles
for a new magic

STEP 2
Conscious experiences as meaning in life

I began my search for meaning in life by asking, what is it we value most? What is it about us, today, that seems most precious? That's what our new magic should be about.

I came up with four answers, four principles. I'll run through them in this and the next three steps.

The first principle involves conscious experience. Deep down, I feel, that's what matters most to us. It's conscious experience that puts us in touch with everything else, with our thoughts and feelings, our memories and our hopes for the future, art and science, and so on. It's our doorway to everything else.

But is it just that, a doorway, and nothing more? For some people I think that's true, it's enough they're just alive, there isn't anything special to call consciousness apart from that. It's just comes with being alive. When I talk about conscious experiences I'm talking about more than that. I'm talking about being conscious of being conscious.

For some people, that's what happens when they meditate, they monitor what they're conscious of, and can control it and direct it. For others, it may be what they go on holiday for, a heightened sense of wonder and excitement at seeing and doing new things. Then, consciousness is what, in you, makes being alive different when you're on vacation. When you show people your vacation photos, what you want to share with them is not just what you saw or did. They've seen pictures of the Eifel Tower before. What you want to share with them is the conscious experience you had, being there, seeing or doing that. You're saying, "I was there, I had the experience of being there, it was intense."

Now, imagine, once you return home you can't turn that off that heightened consciousness. Instead of life being just a blur, you have vivid conscious experiences like that all the time. And actually you probably do. Think back over just the past few days, and what stands out are particular memories that you remember because of what you were thinking or feeling. That's what I mean by conscious experiences. For me, they're what matter most in life, they're what make life most precious. We aren't robots, we're human beings, what makes us different from robots is, we have conscious experiences.

For me, it's our awareness of conscious experiences, first and foremost, that makes human life meaningful, that makes us wonderful.

STEP 3
Enhanced consciousness

For my second principle I asked myself, what conscious experiences am I talking about? Each one, just as it comes? Or can I improve them somehow?

If we have on average ten conscious experiences each day, in the next 20 years we've over 70,000 more conscious experiences to look forward to. And what is it about those conscious experiences that makes them seem precious? It's how rich and rewarding we can imagine them being, like those we have on vacation.

How can we make our remaining conscious experiences richer? I can think of only one way. We can enrich our future conscious experiences only by what we make ourselves conscious of in the present. That's all we have direct control over.

And not just by enjoying ourselves as much as we can in the present so we'll have some good memories to look back on. It might mean just the opposite—it might mean putting those tens of thousands of future conscious experiences first. Think of it as like bundling up to take a bracing walk because of how good you know you'll feel afterwards. Or think of it as like putting money into a savings account. By sacrificing something today you can give yourself richer conscious experiences tomorrow.

So the first two principles in my new magic are, what's most precious for each of us is knowing we've thousands more conscious experiences to come, and that we can enrich them by what we decide to make ourselves conscious of today.

STEP 4

"Meaning in life" involves meaning

What is consciousness? I experience it as a flow of meanings. So one way we can make our conscious experiences deeper and richer over a lifetime is by gathering more and better "meanings."

Fortunately, there's no shortage of them. Meanings multiply like rabbits. Put a couple of meanings together and they'll combine to make new meanings. Here's an example. From the meanings "mother" and "father" we came up with the meanings "Mother country" and "Fatherland." Our mother country is where we were nurtured, by our mothers, our Fatherland is the territory we'll fight alongside our fathers to defend the borders of.

Because we can associate meanings like this to make more meanings, as long as we live we'll keep gathering new meanings. And since consciousness runs on meanings, it's mainly through these meanings that our future conscious experiences become enriched.

So principle number three is, to enrich consciousness we have to understand and manage, not science, but meanings. That's what we're after—more and better meanings in life.

STEP 5
Meanings come from how we evolved

The fourth principle in my new magic is about where meanings come from. It's not hard to see how they multiply, as meanings "mother" and "father" multiplied into Mother country and Fatherland. But what happens if you trace chains of meanings back in the other direction? Where do meanings like Mother and Father originate?

I believe, when we trace chains of meaning back, we'll find they originate in our animal nature, the nature we were born with. My fourth principle is, all the meanings we gather throughout life originate in meanings programmed into us by evolution.

Look what had to happen for us to find anything meaningful. First we had to evolve ways to read the world around us—fortunately our brains come with tools for judging the distance and direction of things. Then we got senses to give those things color and shape. We evolved ways of managing time—you can remember the past, you can be conscious in the present, you can predict the future. Now, able to read space and time, we're ready to give things meaning. We acquire sensations such as fear and desire. We're now prepared for more particular meanings, like mother and father.

Only then can we come up with new meanings like Mother country and Fatherland and tools like being able to reason, to reach conclusions and make decisions. We first had to evolve this deep framework of meanings before we could build over it the rich forest of meanings consciousness runs on. That's why, to find new meaning in life, we first have to understand how we evolved.

So those are the four basic principles behind my new magic. First, what matters to us most is how rich and satisfying our future conscious experiences can be. Second, we can make those future conscious experiences richer by what we make ourselves conscious of today. Third, because conscious experiences consist of meanings, to make them richer we have to think in terms of meanings. And fourth, to understand meanings we have to trace them back to their origin in how we evolved.

Let's go.

SECTION 2

A dark magic blocks our path

In this Section I probe into a magic, associated with science, that denies us the principles our magic is based on.

STEP 6
Telling magics apart

I thought this would be easy. Once I had my four principles I thought I'd be free to come up with a new magic and use it to find new meaning in life.

But immediately I ran into an obstacle. Blocking my way was today's science, with a dark magic it comes with. Before we could go on I realized we first had to understand this other magic and figure out how to get around it. That's what Section 2 will be about.

This dark magic says we don't have control of consciousness. We can't think and do whatever we want. Here's how I understand the principles behind it:

> All that's real is physical matter and the physical processes that act on it.

> Everything that happens is determined by the laws of physics so everything we think and do in the present moment has been determined for us by what's already happened.

> Consciousness may exist in some way—even scientists experience it—but it isn't physical, so it can't make anything physical happen, Communications between consciousness and the brain can go only one way, from the brain to consciousness. Consciousness can't tell our brains what to do.

Everything we do and think is arrived at in our brains, which are purely physical, before we can become conscious of them. Any impression we have that we can decide what to think or do, consciously—that we have free will—is an illusion.

Everything we'll ever become conscious of in the future has already been decided for us by the laws of physics acting on the physical state of things in the present.

Do you see why these principles are such a barrier to us? They completely contradict the four principles I'm trying to make magic out of. If communication can go only from brain to consciousness, but not the other way, then us choosing what to be conscious of can't make any difference to what actually happens. No matter what we make ourselves conscious of today, it can't make any difference to what we'll be conscious of in the future. It can't do anything to enrich it.

Of course, if everyone agreed with me that this scientific magic was dark there'd be no problem. But many people see this dark magic as a white magic. They'll say it's our magic, that gives consciousness control over what we do, that's dark and they'll want us to give it up and accept theirs.

How can you tell if something you're presented with is a dark or a white magic? I think, by how it feels. I'm going to give you an opportunity, now, to compare how the two magics feel.

Magic number 1.

Listen for a moment to the sounds around you.
Now look around. Look for whatever's colored
green. Now look for whatever's colored red.
Look at some distant object, focus on it as
sharply as you can. What details do you see?
Now widen your vision and take in the scene as
a whole. These are just a few of the thousands
of different ways we can pay attention to what's
around us. You can direct your attention any
way you consciously decide to. Didn't you just
do that?

Would you like this kind of experience to
become deeper and richer the longer you live?
What could you think of now, that will make
your future conscious experiences richer? Can
you imagine thinking about this and coming up
with more ideas for how to make the experience
of being conscious more rewarding?

Magic number 2.

Well, actually, of course, that isn't possible.
You didn't direct your attention consciously just
now, your attention simply did what it was told
to. Everything you and I think is already
determined ahead of time. Your conscious
experience is simply a result of what's already
gone on in your brain, and that's all physical
and chemical. All your thinking happens first in
your brain, strictly according to the laws of
physics, it's all determined. Thinking you can
choose, consciously, what to be conscious of,
that's just an illusion. It's impossible. You're as

mechanical as everything else in the universe.

You've no control over your conscious experiences, so thinking you can enrich your future conscious experiences by what you think today, that's just an illusion. You're better off just realizing that, whatever you do, whatever you think, there's no way you can enrich your future conscious experiences. They'll be whatever they'll be, you can't have any effect on them by what you think or do in the present.

I've just tried to help you experience two different ways of being conscious of yourself and of what it means to be alive. If I asked you to, which would you choose? The one where everything you do is determined for you by physics, where you've no free will?

Here's a way to think about that choice. Think of consciousness as a window, a window that's all around you. In it you can see everything: all your feelings, all your thoughts, everything.

Set into that window, in front of you, is a smaller window, like a TV screen. That smaller window shows you everything that's physical, everything alive, all the people you know. That smaller window represents the world outside you, of places and things.

Then you notice, in one corner of that small window there's a third even-smaller window, the size of a cell phone screen. In that third window everything's lined up in neat order, everything can be neatly accounted for. That is the world according to science.

Look a little closer and you see there's someone peering in at you through that window and shouting something. He'd trying to tell you nothing's real except what you can see through that little window.

That's what I think. Consciousness is a lot bigger than science. Rules that have been found to apply when you look through that little science window don't necessarily apply to all of conscious experience. I think we're free to choose whichever of those two magics feels better to us. I prefer magic number 1, where we're free, to some extent at least, of determination by physics, free to make our own choices.

If you preferred that magic too, the one that lets you choose what to be conscious of today so you can enrich your conscious experiences tomorrow, this book is for you.

Steps in Section 3 will lead us around science's dark magic, to the white magic we want. But in the rest of this Section I'm going to point out why that dark magic of science has such a hold over us. Believe me, it has more of a hold over you than you realize. Understanding it better will help you shake it off.

STEP 7
Origin of this dark magic

The belief we're physically determined, that
everything in the universe is determined ahead of
time by the laws of physics, has had a very long run.
Nearly three thousand years ago it showed up in
Greece, as atomism. The entire universe, including
us, consisted of nothing but atoms bouncing around in
space. Everything was the result of how those atoms
collided and joined together.

Nearly a thousand years later, Christianity at first
seemed to save us from atomism. But then it had a
change of heart—because God knows everything, he
must already know everything we'll ever think or do,
so that's already "pre-destined." Once again,
everything we thought and did was determined

Another thousand years later this pre-destination
got swept away by modern science. But science soon
reduced the universe to a clockwork "mechanism"
and, in that mechanistic universe, everything became
determined in advance by Newton's laws of
mechanics. Physical determinism was back, again!

Who would save us from it this time?

All along Christianity had been suppressing the
ancient magics of astrology and alchemy. Then, with
the Renaissance, those magics sprang back to life, to
challenge both Christianity and Newton. A couple of

centuries later they inspired the Liberty, Equality and Brotherhood of the French Revolution.

But the horror of the Revolution made magic once again turn from seeming white to seeming very dark. Ancient magic and witchcraft became what we came to call "black magic."

Why bother with such old history? Because magics are like furnaces forging new meanings. Without those meanings we'd still be hunter gatherers on the African savannah. It's through magics that people have always come up with the meanings that mattered most to them. And those meanings never die, they linger on in words we use today, like destiny and fate. If we hadn't inherited those words it might never occur to us to ask, what is the meaning of life? Magics matter.

Next, we'll bring the story up to date.

STEP 8
Dark magic today

Where do today's main meanings come from?

After the French Revolution the most pressing problem was how to prevent such horror from ever happening again. A Frenchman, August Comte, came up with a solution, a way to establish facts everyone would have to agree on. No more disagreements, no more revolutions.

His solution began with scientific experiment. If you arrived at facts through scientific experiment, everyone else would have to accept them too, once they carried out the same experiment. He gave new meaning to what it meant to "prove" something.

But also important was how he said you had to account for what you found—"Reductionism." Reductionism meant accounting for the results of your experiments in terms of more fundamental sciences. Anything to do with human nature you had to account for in terms of biology, anything to do with biology you had to account for in terms of chemistry, which then had to be accounted for in terms of physics and mathematics.

Comte called this Positivism. He offered it as a new white magic. And it was very successful. Very quickly Positivism became the basis for modern science. Modern science still refers to itself as Positivist science.

But inside this new way of practicing science was a seed of that old dark magic. Reductionism meant that every explanation for why things happened, every theory about them, had to be reduced, ultimately, to physics and mathematics. There we were, back at physical determinism. Once again someone's come up with a magic telling us we can't arrive at our decisions consciously. We can't consciously choose what to be conscious of today, so as to enrich our future conscious experiences. That's my goal, remember?

Comte promised that "Positivism" would usher in continual scientific progress. But, in Britain, standing in the way of that progress was the established Church of England. Church and science got pitted against each other. The church's greatest power lay in its authority based on God being Creator. But once you got used to "reducing" everything to math and physics, whatever wasn't physical, like Gods and angels, stopped seeming real. Down went the church. Within a few decades, "doubt" about Christianity swept through Britain, and then America.

Victory for Positivist science. But if what wasn't physical wasn't "real," what did that say about consciousness, creativity and free will? They weren't physical, so they couldn't be real either. They were just something the purely physical brain did.

Physical determinism was back with a vengeance. It's still with us.

STEP 9
Today's champions of this dark magic

Why is that dark magic still so influential? What keeps it alive? Some very influential people just seem to like it. They like how it feels.

Here's what Susan Blackmore, author of a college textbook on consciousness, "Consciousness: An Introduction," says of the experience of having free will: "I long ago set about changing the experience. I now have no feeling of acting with free will, although the feeling took many years to ebb away." Now she wants to give up all conscious experience altogether: "As for giving up the sense of an inner conscious self altogether—this is very much harder. I just keep on seeming to exist. But though I cannot prove it, I think it is true that I don't." (edge.org/response-detail/11615). She's making physical determinism her meaning in life and goes on speaking tours around the US and UK advising everyone else to do the same.

Here's another book on consciousness, *Breaking the Free Will Illusion for the Betterment of Mankind*. This author also seems to enjoy feeling he's determined, and thinks we all would. "I didn't write this book of my own free will," he says. "The need and desire to write this book to disseminate the information within to others was one that came about through long processes that stem from events I had no control over." And of us, readers of his book, "Of course whether (or not) people listen to the reasoning in this book won't be freely chosen. Rather it will be determined…" So as far as he's concerned he had no conscious choice in what he wrote, and you the reader can't consciously choose whether or not to read it.

Here's the American philosopher Daniel Dennett, author of several influential books on consciousness. "Our minds are just what our brains non-miraculously do…. We are each made of mindless robots and nothing else, no non-physical, non-robotic ingredients at all." He seems entirely comfortable with this magical belief and has devoted his career to promoting it.

How seriously should you take physicalists like that? Let's take Sam Harris as an example. He wrote a book titled "Free Will" in which he happily concludes that "the facts tell us that free will is an illusion." He believes he doesn't have free will, what he's conscious of has been determined by physics. So there's no way he could enrich his future conscious experiences by choosing what to be conscious of today. But note this: for him consciousness isn't physical so there's no way his purely physical brain can know anything about his conscious experience, such as whether it feels richer at some times than others. He believes we don't even have a self, to consider these issues, all we have is a succession of experiences in the present moment. "All we have is now—and now—and now" he says in a Youtube video (Search youtube.com for "Why you're wasting your life away.")

To me, physicalism like that is a psychosis. Look at what he's saying. First, everything he's telling us is as physically determined as a shower of pebbles tumbling off a cliff—there can't be any conscious judgment behind it. Second, because consciousness isn't physical it can't communicate anything to the brain which is purely physical, so there's no way his brain can know what his consciousness is like. So what does he think he's doing, standing at a lectern telling us about free will and consciousness?

This seems to me a very dark magic. Yet it's heavily promoted. Is that effective? A recent Scientific American survey found almost half of readers responding—49%—believing we don't have free will. By now, a few years later, probably a majority of them believe everything we think and do is determined according to the laws of physics. The dark magic of determinism is widespread and growing. It's spreading like a virus throughout our universities.

STEP 10
Who's going to save us this time?

You may wonder why I'm making such a fuss about physical determinism. You may think it has nothing to do with you, you're free to think whatever you like.

But almost certainly you've fallen under the spell of the latest version of this same dark magic. By believing in a theory put forward by one of Comte's followers you've almost certainly fallen for that same old magic of physical determinism, that denies you free will and conscious choice.

That follower of Comte was Charles Darwin. He was so impressed by Comte's ideas he assumed even evolution must be given a reductionist explanation. The explanation he came up with he called "natural selection." It may have the world "natural" in it, but the mechanism he proposed was purely mechanical, physical. At first, a theory giving humans a purely physical origin seemed too shocking to publish. But in just 20 years the scientific community had so accepted Comte's ideas that Darwin felt he could publish his "Origin of Species." Through it he convinced the world of science that even we humans are a product of purely physical processes.

Ever since, scientists have felt justified in applying reductionism to every aspect of human nature. Through them Darwin has turned almost all of us into believers in that old dark magic. Because we're the product of a purely physical process, whatever we think and do must be determined by the laws of physics.

Where's help going to come from this time?

This time help is coming from the top. Some of the world's most eminent evolutionists have joined together to spread "doubt," this time doubt about the mechanism for evolution Darwin came up with, natural selection. Listen to this: "Below, you will find a list of researchers and authors who have, in one way or another, expressed their concerns regarding natural selection's scope and who believe that other mechanisms are essential for a comprehensive understanding of evolutionary processes."

"Concerns about natural selection's scope"? What concerns. They don't say. So I will. In the next Step I'll look at Darwinism, in some detail. If that's more detail than you want, skip over that Step to the one after.

STEP 11
A close look at Darwinism

Here's Darwin's big idea:

> In any species of living creatures, some of them will have characteristics that make them particularly well adapted to their environment.

> That will make those individuals more likely to survive to reproduce and pass those characteristics on to future generations.

> The result is, over time the species will become increasingly well adapted to its environment, until it has enough new characteristics to qualify as a new species.

Simple. Obvious. But there's a problem. Because natural selection favors some characteristics at the expense of others, as time goes on some of them will get lost altogether, there'll be less and less variation left for natural selection to work on, and eventually it'll stop working. To provide new variation, natural selection got teamed up with "genetic mutation." It's that combination, called "the modern synthesis," that's the basis of today's scientific theory of evolution.

What's wrong with that? What's wrong is, it's mainly magic.

Let's start with genetic mutation. "Mutation" means random damage. Because our chromosomes are such long molecules they're constantly cracking and breaking. Random damage to such a complex blueprint will nearly always be harmful. So as this damage accumulates, generation after generation, creatures defined by these damaged blueprints will become less and less fit, and the species will quickly go extinct. That's genetic mutation—damage to genes, accumulating generation by generation, leads rapidly to extinction.

But I left out the magic. Here it is. It comes in two parts. One is called "beneficial mutations." It says, when you damage a very complicated blueprint, at random, just by the laws of chance the result could very occasionally be an improvement. What scientific evidence is there for this theory? None, as far as I can tell except, in the words of the theory's author, "Such beneficial mutations may reasonably be supposed to occur." That's all the proof he or anyone else gives for their existence. In other words, it's magic. It's magic introduced to make the theory work. Once you accept this magic, then along with all those harmful mutations you'll assume every now and again there'll be one that's "beneficial."

But by itself that won't make any difference, there'll still be many more harmful mutations than beneficial ones, and once again the species will rapidly go extinct. To go from harmful genes being in the majority to beneficial genes being in the majority you need another piece of magic—a process that gets rid of all the harmful mutations, while keeping all the mutations that are beneficial, with 100% efficiency.

According to the author of this theory, Ronald Fisher, that process is Darwin's natural selection.

Unfortunately, as even he admits, natural selection is nowhere near 100% efficient, it's only about 1% efficient. To me (but apparently not to him) that means harmful genes will still remain in the majority and the species will once again go extinct, just 1% slower.

Obviously, without those two magical principles—some damage to chromosomes being beneficial and natural selection being 100% efficient—the theory doesn't work. But, for some people, having the modern synthesis deny us free will is so important they're prepared to overlook all the magic and call it science.

Of course natural selection must work some of the time. If a particular gene already comes in two different versions, some individuals having one, some the other, then as the environment changes one version of that gene may be favored over the other. For example, a gene in birds may come in different versions coding for different kinds of beak. Birds with different shaped beaks count as "races" within the species. Then, as the food available to them changes, the "race" with the version of that gene best suited to the new food is more likely to survive, and that bill shape will become more common.

This is called "Microevolution." It's the kind of evolution Darwin was talking about. His subtitle for his "Origin of Species…" was "The Preservation of Favoured Races in the Struggle for Life." It's the easy kind of evolution to account for. What it can't account for is "Macroevolution"—the creation of species, with entirely new genes. That's what most needs accounting for, and that's what today's scientific theory can't do. It can account for selection among different versions of the same gene, different races, but it can't account for the creation of entire combination of genes working together, like you'd need to code for an elephant's trunk.

But besides that, even if it did work there'd be an even bigger problem. Even if it did work, we wouldn't like the kind of creature it made us.

That's because of the merciless logic behind natural selection. In each generation more creatures are born than are needed, only a few creatures have to survive long enough to reproduce themselves, all the rest must die first. So the characteristics that natural selection would pass on to future generation would be those helping individuals survive at the expense of their fellows. And which characteristics will they be? Not characteristics for being slightly better adapted to the environment. No, they'll be skill in murdering one's fellow creatures, raping potential mates, and practicing infanticide on others' young. Logic tell us, if Darwin's natural selection was the mechanism of evolution, it would be primarily genes for those characteristics that would have come to define future generations.

But that's just not how living creatures are. Even wolves aren't like that, they collaborate in hunting and tenderly care for each other's cubs. Living creatures just don't show signs of having been created according to the "just so story" of the modern synthesis. We just don't seem to be what you'd get if we'd evolved along the lines of science's purely physical and deterministic theory.

That list of Darwin-doubters I mentioned in the previous Step appears on a website called "The Third Way of Evolution." By that they mean, some other way than either today's scientific theory, or Creationism—the special creation of species by God. So what is this third way? They all agree on doubting the modern scientific theory of evolution but they've no idea what to replace it with.

I have a suggestion. I tell you about in the Section coming up.

SECTION 3

A new white magic

In an idea proposed by an early
pioneer of evolutionary theory
I find a signpost pointing in
another direction

STEP 12
A new white magic promises new meanings

Auguste Comte's Positivism—his combination of scientific experiment and reductionism—was a white magic when he created it. But in time, as most magics do, it just wore out. A magic that solved one problem at one moment in time—enforcing agreement on facts—became a problem—one more support for determinism, that today we need another magic to solve.

Where can we go, to find inspiration for a new magic?

While the horrors of the French Revolution were discrediting the ancient magics of astrology and alchemy, the first full account of evolution was published in England by another Darwin, Charles Darwin's grandfather, Erasmus Darwin. In the 100-page account of evolution that he titled "Zoonomia," Erasmus suggested several ways living creatures could evolve. Three of them were later championed by others to become the main theories of evolution we know today, including the natural selection of his grandson Charles.

But one of his suggestions has remained unexploited. We've only recently been able to make sense of it. Erasmus was something of a poet, here's how he put it: "… in the great length of time, since the earth began to exist…would it be too bold to imagine, that;"

all warm-blooded animals have arisen from one living filament

- possessing the faculty of continuing to improve by its own inherent activity,
- delivering down those improvements by generation to its posterity.

In other words, could the origin of species be a "living filament" able to direct its own evolution?

Today his "living filament" seems an astonishingly accurate prediction of something that wouldn't be discovered for another two centuries, the genome.

By "the genome" we mean all a creature's genes. In us that's all the information needed to grow a human being from a single cell to an adult. In a microbe its genome can be a single molecule, a single "filament" made up of a string of DNA subunits. But as living creatures evolved and became more complicated the genome grew too, from just a few hundred genes to tens of thousands. We carry a copy of our genome in the nucleus of every cell in our body, broken up into a few dozen DNA molecules, our chromosomes.

It's by the genes that make up their genomes that we tell species apart. A species' genes are what define it. They're what tell it what kind of creature to be

Notice what Erasmus says about the genome. He calls it a filament, and that's true, it is a filament or a collection of filaments, long linear molecules. And as he said, it is alive, it's part of a living cell and each time a cell divides it divides too. And, as he said, improvements built into it, in the form of changes to genes, will get passed down through successive generations, to eventually define new species. So all this is literally true of the genome.

But note what else he says—the genome itself can "improve," and it can do so "through its own inherent activity." In other words, the genome can direct its own evolution, it can all by itself be what makes species evolves. Could genomes, he's asking, be what drives evolution?

What does this have to do with our magic?

Remember the four principles I've already proposed? What's most precious in our lives is conscious experience. We can enrich our future conscious experiences by what we consciously choose to make ourselves conscious of today. Doing so will involve managing meanings. Most of our meanings originated in how we evolved. Erasmus Darwin's fourth great insight may lead us to the theory of evolution we need to understand how those meanings could have evolved.

Let's look a little deeper.

STEP 13

Implications of this other Darwin's thinking

Erasmus Darwin's suggestion, that what drives evolution is the genome, may not seem very promising at first. But from it you can draw some remarkable implications. In fact, it can turn your world upside down. It can account for what makes us so wonderful.

What we know about ourselves above all is, every so often we're conscious and creative. That tells us something not only about us but about the World we live in. It tells us it's a kind of world that consciousness and creativity can exist in. Since that's so, since they exist in us and we're part of the world, they could exist elsewhere in the world besides us. They could exist in the genome, too. The genome could already have something corresponding to our consciousness, our being creative, our having free will, that it passes on to us. After all, we don't make ourselves conscious and creative. We wouldn't know how. It's something that happens to us. It could be, we get them from whatever they correspond to in the genome.

Where else could we have got them from? I can't think of any more likely place.

Looking at evolution this way, what's really

important about it isn't what happened to us, it's what had to happen first to the genome. First the genome had to evolve, to become intelligent, conscious and creative. Only then could it create us, in the process embedding in us some of its own talents, what in us we experience as our minds. So what we call "evolution" is really two processes. First, the genome had to evolve. Then it created us. These could be two entirely different processes, each with its own kind of wisdom.

And our meanings? What does logic say about them? That they originated as parts of the genome's own wisdom, that it built into us, for us to think with, like Lego blocks an adult gives to a child for it to play at making something.

If the world really is like that, then we need to take account of two kinds of processes active in it: physical processes acting on matter, and evolutionary processes acting on living creatures.

How can that turn our world upside down? Because we can come up with new answers to questions. For example, what is thinking? Everyone agrees, it isn't physical. What is it, then? If thinking isn't something physical involving physical forces, then it could involve this other kind of process that we've just arrived at, involving evolution. What that suggests is, thinking is our thoughts evolving, each thought evolving into the next. Our thoughts could evolve into one another the way species of living creatures evolve into one another. And because it isn't a purely physical process, thinking won't necessarily be determined by laws of physics.

And consciousness? It could be an experience automatically conjured up when thoughts evolve into one another. As our thoughts evolve into each other we experience that as consciousness. Then both we, and the genome, can be genuinely creative, can have free will, can choose what to think about today for the sake of what we want to be conscious of tomorrow.

That's a view of the world I find buried in Erasmus Darwin's fourth theory. It's a new plan for how the world is put together.

What else can it tell us?

STEP 14
A new theory of evolution

If thinking is an evolutionary process, can that tell us how living creatures evolve?

That's too big a stretch. Let's start with an easier question. What's going to happen when the genome "thinks"?

Maybe something like what happens when we think.

When we think—when we remember something for example—we make changes to our brain cells. Later, from those same brain cells, we can recall that memory. This means conscious experiences can read themselves into physical matter—brain chemistry— and those physical changes can be read back into consciousness. We do it all the time.

Suppose something like that is true of the genome—suppose when it thinks it makes changes to its "brain." Now remember, its "brain" is the genes it consists of, and genes are what define a species. So, if it thinks the way we do, merely by thinking the genome can make changes to the genes it corresponds to, and changes to genes is what brings a new species into existence.

I know at first this seems implausible. Mere thinking can drive chemical changes? But that does seem to be how our thinking works, we can deliberately, consciously, think memories—think chemical changes—into our brain cells. If that process can take place in us, there's no logical reason why it can't take place in the genome. Imagine the genome bringing to mind—recalling—the genes that make up a species, re-thinking them, and storing them back as changed genes. That would solve an old mystery. What is a species? Species turn out to be, in essence, thoughts in the minds of a genome.

STEP 15
Life, a community of minds

Those of us who aren't scientists are used to distinguishing between matter and mind. In this new worldview we'll still make that distinction. But now we're adding a new kind of mind, the mind of the genome.

Which genome? This one, at the end of my finger, or that one, on my nose? I'm going to suggest to you, it's all of them working together. Genomes can read each other's "minds" and arrive at decisions together. They're responsible for managing life at every level from the nucleus of a single cell, up through an organism's various tissues, to the organism itself, to species and all the way up to entire Kingdoms of life.

In other words, all of life, at every level, is maintained by the intelligences of genomes, working together.

This may seem crazy at first. But the living world is hard to explain otherwise. Think of a whale growing from an infant to an adult 100 feet long. As it grows its various parts stay in perfect proportion. The information needed to direct that whale's growth exists in the genome in every cell of its body. But how can all those genomes, separately, direct the growth of a living creature like a whale, over distances of many feet? What else but a community of genomes? What else could maintain a whale's two flippers in perfect symmetry? And they must, because if those flippers grew at different rates we'd see young whales swimming in circles, and we don't.

Here's another puzzle: mammals and molluscs come from very different branches in the tree of life yet they evolved very similar eyes. That suggests information can be exchanged between very different branches of the tree of life? How the living world looks, it's as if there's a community of intelligence operating at every level from the individual cell up to entire living Kingdoms.

So in this new natural philosophy there are three kinds of thing. There are those we're already familiar with—matter, and individual creatures' minds. And there are minds involved in the collective intelligences of genomes.

The ideas I've pulled from Erasmus Darwin may seem like a random hodge-podge. But together they provide us with a coherent account of everything we experience. Here's a quick summary. The purely physical world remains as science tells us it is. But the evolved world is very different. First the genome evolved to become conscious and creative, then it learned how to create species of living creatures in its own image, like us. Into each of us it built some of its own consciousness, creativity, memory, intuition and anticipation. It also built into each of us a framework of meanings, meanings that make up the rails consciousness runs on. Consciousness consists of experiences generated in us by our thoughts as they evolve into one another. Just as our thoughts evolve in our minds, species of living creatures are ideas that evolve in the mind of the genome.

Notice, this is just what today's physical science has the most difficulty explaining. It's much easier to talk about in terms of the new magic. And just having a way to talk about something may be enough, that may be all we need to feel we "understand" it. Science may give us greater understanding of the physical world, these new ideas may give us greater understanding of the living world.

And of ourselves. We're going to need that greater understanding if we're going to use Erasmus' pioneering work to help us locate new meaning in life today.

Magically made wonderful

In this section we learn we're not just magical, we're wonderful.

STEP 16
Kicking the tires of the new magic

For genius in thinking about evolution I turn to Erasmus Darwin. But for a genius with sheer brain power, I go back a century or two earlier, to Galileo. Almost single handed, Galileo turned the natural philosophy of the Middle Ages into the natural philosophy we subscribe to today. Could asking questions as Galileo did help us extend our compass?

Let's imagine what questions Galileo would ask and what kind of logic he'd use to answer them.

Take our chromosomes, for example, they're just long molecules. Could molecules like that support a mind? Well, I imagine Galileo saying, a human brain is made just of molecules, yet it supports a mind. The genome isn't as complex as our brains but it's been evolving for a thousand times as long. It's hard to set a limit to what kind of a mind something like that could support.

Are the genome's molecules long enough to support a mind? Well, they are extremely long. The chromosomes making up my genome, joined end to end in a straight line, would make a molecule longer than I am tall. Think of that, a molecule 6 foot long. That's hard to get one's mind around, even a mind like Galileo's.

Here's how I think he'd tackle that.

Our genes are written out in units of molecular code, four different kinds of them, acting like letters of a four-letter alphabet. Now imagine translating the letters in my 6-foot-long genome into beads of four different colors, one bead for each letter, and stringing them into a necklace of beads strung eight to an inch—that's a pretty tightly strung necklace. As a necklace like that the phrase "have a nice day" would stretch about four inches. The US constitution would stretch about 100 yards. By comparison, my entire genome would stretch 6000 miles, from New York to Tokyo in Japan, 14 hours travel by air. It'd be hard even for Galileo to imagine any limit to what that could code for.

How does the genome code for information? We know how it codes for proteins. It takes three of its molecular units at a time, in different combinations that code for each of 20 amino acids, that then join together and fold up to become proteins. That's OK, that makes mathematical sense. But code for the 20,000 proteins in our bodies takes up only one sixtieth of the genome. How does it code for everything else besides those proteins? Science doesn't yet know.

What else does the genome code for besides proteins? Take a web-spinning spider, for example. That spider knows how to drop down on a strand of silk but to get back up it knows it has to climb back up that strand. It doesn't need to be taught that, it comes into the world knowing about it, about gravity. It also comes into the world knowing about space— for attachment points for its web it has to be able to locate points all lying in a single flat plane. It comes knowing how to spin its species' distinctive web, and how to hide, and then rush out when it detects movements in the web indicating it has trapped some prey, how to inject it with poison and immobilize it with a silk wrapping. It knows how to recognize members of its opposite sex, and what to do to mate and have its eggs hatch. All this information must come coded for in its genome, it has no other source of information to draw on.

So the spider comes into the world knowing a great deal about the world that it's hard to imagine being coded for the same limited way proteins are.

How could information like that be coded for in the genome? Could the genome be a hologram? You can record information on a single sheet of film so as you walk past it you see what looks like a continuous video. Could the genome be a one-dimensional hologram, like that, with all kinds of messages overlapping along it? Probably not, but something like that has to be true for living creatures to be as complex as they are.

How complex are they? What wonders do we know the process of evolution is capable of, that a theory of evolution has to be able to account for?

STEP 17
What can be written in a genome?

Not just the amino acid sequences that make up proteins.

What other kinds of information must a genome like ours code for? And how much information?

Let's start small. Let's look at just how the fur lies on the head of a cat. Cats need unobstructed vision both into the distance to hunt and close up to eat their prey. So that their vision is unobstructed, hairs around their eyes are short and lie flat against the skin, all pointing away from each eye. Hairs thin out in front of the ears, are absent inside the ear, are short and lie flat on the back. On the cat's nose, hairs are absent and they're short around the mouth, except for a few long whiskers.

So the cat genome codes precisely for the hairs covering the cat's face: their length, lie, density, and how stiff they are. Now bear in mind that this precision and complexity of form applies to everything about the cat's body—its eyes, its sense of smell and taste, its heart, lungs, kidneys, liver, digestive enzymes, claw production, muscle attachments to bones and so on. That could be more information than you'd need to run the US army, yet it all must be in there, written in the cat's genome.

What controls how an animal grows from a single

cell to the full-size adult? Take an adult whale, for example, which can be 100 feet long. At school I was told that growth was directed by a succession of chemical gradients, each one inducing the next. But just by swimming all the time a whale would be continuously stirring up those chemical gradients, they wouldn't last very long. So for want of any other explanation I assume it's the genome that manages growth throughout the whale, over distances of 100 feet in length and 25 feet from the tip of one flipper to the tip of the other.

That's all managed precisely in accordance with a tight schedule. So the genome can manage time as well.

And how things work. A whale's heart can be as big as a small car, the valves in it can be as big as garbage-can lids, it can pump half a bathtub-full of blood at a time into a blood vessel one foot across. Now bear in mind that, as a whale grows from just a few cells to its enormous final size, all that heavy equipment had to continue working as it grows without stopping for a second, or the whale would die!

What kind of specs would you have to write to satisfy an engineering challenge like that! You may not know, you may not even be able to imagine them, but instructions for how to do that must already be there, written somehow in the whale's genome.

Finally, replacement of missing parts. Not only can the genome grow all the parts of a living creature as it grows from a single cell into an adult, but when some parts go missing in the adult the genome can also make those parts from scratch, an entirely different process. For example, there's a kind of salamander known as the axolotl. An adult axolotl can be up to a foot long. Such an adult can regrow large bits of itself: its lower jaw, the retina in its eyes, its ovaries, kidneys, heart, lungs, spinal cord, and large chunks of its brain. So its genome knows not only how to grow each part of an adult axolotl as it grows from a single cell, it knows how to identify almost any part that missing and remake it from scratch, an altogether different process.

But then, its genome is ten times as long as ours, room for a lot of spare-parts information. We lost that. But we gained other talents in its place. Let's look at what makes us special.

STEP 18
Take us, please

An axolotl is an amphibian. We're mammals, a much-more-recently evolved kind of animal. So we should be at least as wonderful as an axolotl, and even more complicated.

To get an idea how complicated we are, compare us to a robot. To control robots scientists had to develop a succession of computer languages, each one building on the one before. Only with that stack of programming languages in place can you say to the robot "grasp the green globe and drop it in the black box." Coming up with languages to get that far has taken engineers decades of intense study.

Yet a mother can tell her child "Pick up all your toys and drop them in the box behind you" and he'll understand.

That gives us some idea of the complexity of programming that each of us comes with, built into our genome. Just being able to pick something up and put it down is a miracle. Yet we can do so much more. The engineering built into our genome is way more awesome that we can comprehend.

Take orgasm. Somehow even a coordinated tangle of feeling and behavior like that can be written into a genome. So even feelings are a real-enough part of this world for them to get written into a creature's genome whenever the process of evolution needs to.

Creation of a creature like us is a staggering achievement. We are wonderful, each of us, by being such a creature, and the genome is wonderful for being able to create such creatures. That is the truth that only today, with our understanding of the role of the genome, we can appreciate, that all philosophies must from now on take into account. Only today can we appreciate the brilliance of Erasmus Darwin's proposal involving a "living filament" over two centuries ago. It can reveal to us just how wonderful we really are.

How wonderful is that?

STEP 19
The magnificent book of life

The study of other living creatures suggests that, being living creatures ourselves, we too are wonderful. But do we feel wonderful? If not, why not?

I can be inspired by Galileo to follow the path of clear cold reason wherever it leads me, as he did. But he in turn was inspired by Ancient Roman humanism, to see human nature as magnificent, full of such wonderful capabilities as clear cold reason. If we intend to make our future conscious experiences wonderful, we too need to be inspired to believe human nature can be magnificent, today.

Where can we turn for our inspiration? To the magnificent book of life, as written all around us by the genome. For a measure of how wonderful we are let's look at how wonderful some of the genomes' other creations are.

For an example of this magnificence let's turn to insects. A lot of the machinery that makes an insect work is built into its skin. That's the hard rigid outer covering that most of its muscles are attached to and pull on. That rigid skin has holes in it for air to diffuse through into a network of passages throughout its body. Skin covers its antennae and frames the lenses for its eyes. Yet some insects every so often shed that skin. Under it they've grown a new skin, along with new attachments for muscles, new holes for circulating air, coverings for its antennae and the lenses covering its eyes, all its bristles and hairs, even its wings and attachments for the muscles that power them.

At first the new skin is soft and the insect can't move or breathe, but in a few hours the new skin has hardened and works just like the old skin. That's like a swiss army knife every so often shedding all its tools and blades and growing a new set, larger but otherwise exactly the same. It's hugely wonderful.

Now let's examine some of the ingenious machinery behind these wonders. In some insects a caterpillar transforms into a larva, which then transforms into an adult with fully-formed legs and wings. Buried in the larva are small flat disks that carry, in a series of concentric circles, all the information needed to form a leg or a wing. When they're needed those disks move to where they belong and stretch out from the center to one side to form all a leg or a wing's components. That's like a vanilla ice cream coming as a small disk like a dime with a brown center and a white surround, you'd make the ice cream by pulling the brown center out to become a cone, followed by the white surround expanding to become the ice cream. It's a wonderful piece of engineering.

Now, bear in mind we're full of engineering as wonderful as that. As bodies, we are just as wonderful.

STEP 20
A dive into ontology and theology

Prepared to take a deep dive? If not, skip over this to the next section.

Ontology. That's arguments about what the world consists of. Here we ask questions like, is there just matter? Or is there both matter and mind? In this book I compare "ontologies" in terms of kinds of processes. Are there only physical and chemical processes. Or are there in addition other kinds processes, found only in living creatures, that to some extent can defy the laws of physics.

Can we tell which of these worlds we actually live in? Not yet, it's still a matter of opinion, of personal judgment.

Here's the critical question: what difference would it make if there were some processes that could defy the laws of physics? Novelties would pop up that you couldn't predict in terms of purely physical processes acting on prior events. Is that true of our world? That's where opinions differ. What some people think are novelties other people dismiss as simply the results of physical processes. For example, nature: the evolution of species and how organisms develop from embryos to adults. Nowadays these are referred to together as "evo-devo." So the question resolves into: Has evo-devo created novelties?

That seems a simple question. Let's consider some examples. How about the appearance on Earth of the first living cell? How about that cell evolving into the far more complex kind of cell we find in our own bodies? How about the evolution of a simple microbe, with a thousand or so genes, into elephants and giraffes with genes by the millions? Are these "genuine" novelties, or could you have predicted them from the action of the laws of physics alone?

I'm biased. To me there couldn't be anything more novel, creative, less bound by the laws of physics, than the appearance over time on Earth of new kinds of living species and what happens during an organism's development. However we define creativity, that has to be its prime example. Whatever processes are responsible for evolution, they are by this definition creative. So in my ontology, there are in the world besides purely physical processes also the creative processes responsible for evolution. That's the source of any creativity we have. It's a characteristic that evolved in us.

Arguing for the other ontology are writers of today's biology textbooks. They insist nature (evo-devo) isn't creative at all. It's simply the result of purely physical processes—the mechanisms behind today's evolutionary theory given enough time to work their magic. We're assured science has proved that nature is not creative, though that's not actually true. Science can't yet measure creativity, so it can't tell which of us is right. Yet that ontology, that all processes are purely physical, is behind how evo-devo is taught in schools and how we may talk about it in public.

Let's come up for air for a moment. Are you

creative? Of course you are. Then creativity is a property of the world you're a part of. You're simply one more instance of nature being creative. There, does that help you decide?

Now another dive. Into religion. Am I proposing making genomes into a new kind of god?

I don't think so. As far as we know genomes exist only here on Earth so they're not infinite like the Christian God. And they're not eternal, they've existed along with the Earth for only a third as long as the universe has existed. And they certainly aren't infallible. 99% of all species of creatures have gone extinct, their genomes along with them.

And, most of all, genomes' main uses for their creatures are as vehicles to carry the genomes around, and to be food to sustain other genomes' creatures, to be fodder for each other. So genomes don't care about their creations individually. They've no interest in carrying on a personal relationship with any one of us.

So, all in all, they're not anything like what we think God should be.

We've been through a succession of ontologies. Christianity said God's responsible for everything. Modern science said everything's determined by physical laws. Erasmus Darwin proposed a third—in addition to non-living matter as science describes it, there's an intelligent process embodied in genomes that then go on to create all living creatures.

Rather than call my magic an ontology or a religion, I like to call it an "as if" theory. The way

evolution looks, to me, it's "as if" my magic is true—
it's an "as if" theory. Richard Dawkins meant
something like that when he titled one of his books
"The Selfish Gene." He didn't mean that genes really
are selfish, he meant that the way evolution looks to
him it's "as if" genes are selfish, competing with one
another to appear in following generations.

So let's think of all this as simply a "heuristic," a
helpful way of thinking about something. That's all
my magic is. I can't prove it's true because we don't
yet know how consciousness evolves, and it could be
centuries before we find out. So within our own
lifetimes we must make do with "as if" theories, and
simply admit when we challenged that, for now,
they're magic.

But even so they can be a source of wisdom.

STEP 21
A preview of wisdom

What difference could all this make? It could lead us to a new source of wisdom we could use to transform human nature. Through studying genomes we'd come to know them as personalities, each with its own creative intelligence and tools. Through studying those tools we could learn how to incorporate them in our own creative intelligences. Then we could make our conscious experience as creative as evolution itself.

Genomes do perform as if they have personalities. For example, trilobites evolved through a fantastic number of highly varied forms for hundreds of millions of years before going extinct, while sharks, which have lasted almost as long, have barely changed. We first need to learn about these different genomes' personalities, special talents, special skills. Through what we learn about the genomes, we may eventually learn about the processes of evolution that gave rise to those genomes and maintain them still, and be able to draw on that wisdom too.

What I'm glimpsing here is a future science. Because it doesn't yet exist I can't bring you any of its wonderful discoveries. But through fiction I can make it a little bit real. I've included such a fiction, a time-travel fantasy, at the end of this book.

SECTION 5

Assembling wisdom

*In this Section we pool all our
resources of wisdom to lay a foundation
for new meaning*

STEP 22
Where else can we look for wisdom?

The first principle of my new magic is, what's most precious in life is our prospect of having many more future conscious experiences. To me that now seems obvious. But when it first occurred to me it felt unfamiliar. Why? Why wasn't it just part of everyday common sense? Haven't people always thought conscious experience was what's matters most in life. Or are we different?

We are different. And in several ways.

Here's one. For nearly two thousand years, people in the West got used to consciousness being a gift from the Christian God, so it didn't need any accounting for. For them, meaning in life came from their relationship with this God and whether, when they died, they'd qualify to enter heaven or hell. It was only a couple of centuries ago, when Christianity began to break down, that people felt the need for a way of accounting for consciousness that didn't involve God.

What have philosophers said about this since then? Not as much as you might expect. Emmanuel Kant thought learning through science what the world is really like would make life meaningful. No, said Hegel, we can't find out from science what the world is really like. All we can do is keep coming up with ideas that help us feel at home in the world, each idea building on the one before. That's like my magics each getting invented in turn, slowly turning from white to black and being succeeded by another. Hegel called that the dialectic process.

Out of that came the phrase "self-conscious"— becoming aware of how we make reality real in the course of our conscious experiences. That phrase— "self conscious"— entered the English language just 200 years ago. So maybe what we call consciousness today is really this self-consciousness, and it's only needed accounting for in the past couple of centuries.

Next, Karl Marx. What most powerfully shapes our self-consciousness, he said, isn't either science or what we think about, it's the work relationships that dominate our lives. And to some extent that seems to be true. Soul-destroying work in factories taught people to see themselves as replaceable cogs in huge machines, that experience then shaping their reality. A century later, as people got used to office work, they would back-up their conscious awareness with address books and diaries, clocks and calendars, and their own personal filing systems. They turned their homes into micro-offices and themselves into micro-managers.

But does identifying with work give us meaning? More recently we've begun shaping our identities around our skill sets. We sign up with LinkedIn to market our skill set under "the brand of you." In Facebook we spruce up our non-work self with the fake-news tricks of public relations, racking up armies of followers to appear popular. On Instagram we enhance our selfies using photo-retouching tricks once confined to advertising agencies. And next? Perhaps in the future there won't be any jobs, and we'll have to find our identity elsewhere. And our meaning.

So much for Marx.

What else is there? As far as modern philosophy is concerned, that leaves mainly existentialism, and according to existentialism life doesn't have any meaning, we have to make it up for ourselves. So much for modern philosophy.

If meaning in life in terms of conscious experiences seems like something we should have been told about but weren't, the main reason is, nobody else knows what to make of it either. Our determination to come up with an answer may be one way we're different.

But there's another way we're different from how people used to be. Our lives are just longer. Human life used to be very precarious and your meaning lay mainly in your own survival and that of your children. But in just over the past century life has become much less precarious. The human lifespan has doubled. A child today soon takes for granted that he or she is likely to live for close to a century. It's one of the most dramatic changes in human history. So instead of mere survival, of ourselves and our families, we naturally seek something else to make our own much longer lives feel worth living.

So we are different from generations before us. We're on our own. To find meaning in life we have to come up with it for ourselves.

STEP 23
Finding meaning in life in consciousness

For the first principle of my new magic I began by identifying meaning with "self-consciousness," with us being aware of our conscious experiences. But notice I settled not on just conscious experience, but on our remaining future conscious experiences. I arrived at that from reading "Thinking, Fast and Slow" by Daniel Kahneman.

As a thought experiment Kahneman asks the reader to think about "your next vacation." It can be as enjoyable as you like, but:

- At the end of the vacation, all pictures and videos will be destroyed.

- You will swallow a potion that will wipe out all your memories of the vacation.

How would this prospect affect your vacation plans, he asks. How much would you be willing to pay for it, relative to a normally memorable vacation?

At first, for me, having no memory of the vacation made it seem valueless, I'd pay nothing for such a vacation, no matter how enjoyable it promised to be. And I was not alone. "My impression from discussing it with people," Kahneman says, "is that the elimination of memories greatly reduces the value of the experience.... some people say that they would not bother to go at all."

But then I realized with a chill that, since I believe all consciousness ends when we die, the same could be said of life itself—after death I would have no memory of any conscious experiences I had while I was alive, just like taking that potion after the vacation. Did that make all of life's conscious experiences worthless? That was unacceptable.

So I changed my answer. Yes, I would value that vacation not only for conscious experiences as I had them but also for the memories I would have each day of what I had enjoyed the day before and for my anticipation of what I'd do in the vacation days still to come. Thinking like that could give meaning to the vacation, and ultimately to life itself.

But there's a crucial difference between the two situations. The vacation would be too short for one day's consciousness to have much impact on the next. But in the course of a long life what one chose to make oneself conscious of each day could enrich all one's future moments. It was this prospect, of ever-more enriched future conscious experiences, that I concluded could make life seem most precious.

Despite knowing all our conscious experiences will cease to exist when we die, anticipating them becoming ever-richer over time can give meaning to life as long as it lasts.

STEP 24

A wisdom of the Ancients

All along there've been traditions of wisdom opposed to physical determinism, that our magic could help us connect us to. For example, our magic is very similar to how the Stoics in Ancient Rome thought about themselves and the world around them.

Generally the Stoics were materialists, as we have become, but they believed that pervading all matter was an extra material substance that they referred to as the World Spirit. It was this World Spirit that made nature creative and maintained order in it. They believed that inside each of us, this World Spirit had embedded a small share of its own wisdom, to guide and inspire us. For us to become modern Stoics all we need do is replace their World Spirit with the intelligence of the genome that, as I've been suggesting, has embedded in each of us some of its own wisdom. To the extent the Stoics believed in fate we believe in laws of physics; like them we believe in reason. "Live according to nature" they said, meaning according both to the laws of the universe and to how those laws expressed themselves. We similarly draw on the creativity of the genome. Ancient Stoicism as a belief system is very similar to our new magic.

The Stoics didn't worship their World Spirit, it wasn't a religion. And it wasn't social, Stoics didn't meet to practice Stoicism. They might go to classes for instruction in stoicism but being a Stoic seems to have been an individual thing, like us subscribing to a classical music station. And their goals were different. Life was much harsher then. Rather than caring about conscious experiences, people cared more about coping with pain and loss. In the long run, though, that wasn't enough and Stoicism gave way to Christianity, with its more intense spirituality in this life and promise of eternal joy in the next.

What can we bring to stoicism? Joy through enriched consciousness. What can we gain from it? Acceptance of death as something not to be troubled about. A sharp distinction between what we have control over, that we can change, and what we don't have control over that we must figure out how to endure. Above all, though, a model for how to develop habits of mind for pursuing whatever goal we have in mind, whether it's to do what's right and just on every occasion, which was their ideal, or to enrich future conscious experiences, which is the one I'm recommending.

The Stoic attitude to life is almost the exact opposite of how most of us think and act today. I do what I'm told to earn a living, we say, to earn time for relaxing with whatever comes along—the internet, TV, shopping. If we decide to learn some new skill it's usually for work, not for developing new habits of mind. The Ancient Stoics believed the opposite. They believed you had to train yourself to do the right thing, to make life the best it could be. They trained themselves strenuously to be the kind of person they wanted to be. In a consumer society it's hard to understand their need for this but if we're serious about finding meaning in life we may need something of the same self discipline. Our goals aren't the same as theirs but we can learn from them how to train ourselves in personal integrity, to achieve our own goals.

STEP 25
A model

You can get a flavor of what it was like for a Stoic to
train him or herself in right thinking from the
exercises the Roman Emperor Marcus Aurelius jotted
down as practice in self discipline. What follows are
extracts from "The Emperor's handbook," translated
by brothers C. Scott and David V. Hicks (Scribner).

Marcus waxes philosophical:

> The light of the sun is one, even when it is
> interrupted by walls, mountains, and a myriad of
> other things. Being is one, even when it is
> dispersed among a host of individual bodies. Life
> is one, even when it is distributed to countless
> natures, each with its own idiosyncratic
> limitations. Mind is one, even when it appears to
> be divided…. You are but a part sustained by the
> whole. Someday your part will be reclaimed by
> what formed it, or rather, through a process of
> change you will re-enter the womb of reason
> through which you were born.
>
> The creative force is a part of everything it
> produces. This should cause us to revere nature
> all the more, as well as to realize that by thinking
> and acting in accord with nature's design and
> will, we tap into the mind of this creative force.
> The cosmic mind is as much a part of us, then, as

it is of the universe, and all the power and knowledge available in the universe are accessible to the man who lives in perfect harmony with nature.

Is it change that you fear? But what can happen without it? What is dearer to nature or more vital to the universe? Look at everything that sustains you. Can you take a warm bath if the wood you burn to heat the water doesn't change? Can you digest your food if it doesn't change? Can any of your needs be met without change? Don't you see, then, that the change resulting in your death is no different and similarly feeds the life of the universe.

What then can guide us through this life? Philosophy, only philosophy. It preserves the inner spirit, keeping it free from blemish and abuse, master of all pleasures and pains, and prevents it from acting without a purpose or with the intention to deceive, ensuring that we lack nothing, whatever others may do or not do.

He practices a stern self-discipline:

One distinguishing mark of the good man: his love and delight in the thread of his own destiny and his refusal to soil or upset with an orgy of sensations the divine spirit dwelling within him, where a serene peace reigns and God is obeyed, and no untrue words are spoken and no unjust deeds performed…. Every hour be firmly resolved… to accomplish the work at hand with fitting and unaffected dignity. Banish from your thought all other considerations. This is possible if you perform each act as if it were your last, rejecting every frivolous distraction, every denial of the rule of reason, every pretentious gesture, vain show, and whining complaint against the decrees of fate… Purge your mind of all aimless and idle thoughts, especially those that pry into the affairs of others or wish them ill.

One man prays, "Help me seduce this woman, "but you pray instead, "Prevent me from lusting after her." Another prays, "Rid me of my enemy," but you pray, "Rid me of the desire to be rid of my enemy." Another, "Do not take my dear child from me," but you, "May I not fear the loss of the child." Turn your prayers in this direction and see what comes of it… In this way you show the world a simple and kindly man, a good neighbor, someone who is indifferent to sensual pleasure and luxuries …

His philosophy promises him control over his own mind, what we might call free will, and joy in having such a mind. He also can second-guess his own thinking processes in quite a modern way.

Nature equips rational beings with the same powers as herself. Just as nature works on whatever opposes or resists her, giving it a place in the necessary order and making it part of herself, so too can a rational being convert every hindrance into material for himself and use it for his own ends.

Worldly circumstances and affairs cannot touch the mind, cannot penetrate it, cannot alter or move it, for the mind alters and moves itself, molding the world in the shape of whatever judgments it pleases the mind to make… Test every thought and sense perception, if possible, by the methods of science, the laws of morality and the rules of logic…. Treat with utmost respect your power of forming opinions, for this power alone guards you against making assumption that are contrary to nature and judgments that overthrow the rule of reason. It enables you to learn from experience, to live in harmony with others, and to walk in the way of the gods…. The happiness of those who want to be popular depends on others; the happiness of those who seek pleasure fluctuates with moods outside their control; but the happiness of the wise grows out of their own free acts….

Nowhere is there a more idyllic spot, a vacation home more private and peaceful, than in one's own mind, especially when it is furnished in such a way that the merest inward glance induces ease…. Take this vacation as often as you like, and to charge your spirit.

The power to live an exemplary life resides in the mind, so long as the mind remains indifferent to the things that are themselves indifferent. But how can it remain indifferent? By carefully examining each thing, both as a whole and in its parts, and by remembering that nothing can oblige us to form an opinion of it. Things don't force themselves upon us. They stand still, while we form judgments of them and write them down, so to speak, on our minds.

"How, at this moment, am I using my mind?" This is a question worth asking all the time. So is this: "How do my words and deeds measure up to the ruling reason with in me? And who owns this mind of mine anyway? An infant? A boy? A woman? A tyrant? A dumb animal? A wild beast?

In the following extract we get a sense of how Stoics studied and celebrated nature:

We should also pause to consider how charming and graceful are the unexpected effects of nature's work. When bread is baking, for example, cracks appear in its crust. Although these would seem to confound the baker's design, they attract our attention and help arouse our appetite. Figs too burst open just when they are best to eat, and olives left on the tree to rot achieve a most exquisite beauty. Similarly, the golden grain's drooping head, the lion's furrowed brow, the boar's foaming snout, and so many other details, if taken out of context, are not all that attractive, but when seen in their natural setting they complete a picture and please the eye.

In this way, the perceptive man, profoundly curious about the workings of nature, will take a peculiar pleasure in everything, even in the humble and ungainly parts that contribute to the making of the whole. The actual jaws of living beasts will delight him as much as their representations by artists and sculptures. With a discerning eye he will warm to an old man's strength or an old woman's beauty, while admiring with cool detachment the seductive charms of youth. The world is full of wonders like these that will appeal only to those who study nature closely and develop a real affinity for her works.

STEP 26
Updating Stoicism

Stoicism is one of the ancient traditions opposed to physical determinism. It's become popular again, with active societies and an international Stoicism week. We can make ourselves an offshoot of modern Stoicism by updating it for our own time.

But update it how?

In two steps. First, with modern physics we can account for everything that's purely physical, such as the tides and weather, we no longer need a World Spirit for that. So we begin by limiting the reach of the World Spirit to the living world. And there, in place of that World Spirit, we install the conscious creative genome. It's this genome that brings creativity to the living world and maintains order in it, and embeds in each of us a small portion of its own wisdom.

I see evolution's wisdom coming in three steps. First, wisdom available to us from the study of individual species of living creatures. We can learn from bats how to move around in the dark, we can learn from spiders how to make pliable materials stronger than steel. From the creatures the genomes have dreamed up we can borrow a host of engineering tips. But ways to enrich consciousness, perhaps not so much.

Step two, what we can learn about genomes themselves. Why do almost all flowers that are pollinated by insects strike us as beautiful? Why do we find beauty in almost all the mating displays of male birds? Is there a single standard of beauty running through the entire tree of genome intelligence that the genomes built into us? Until science tells us otherwise, we can believe that in finding beauty in nature we share some of the genome's own delight in its creative powers. Perhaps we can make part of our own nature. By doing this we could hugely enrich our conscious experience.

Step three will be taking what we learn about the genomes themselves, and from it deducing what must be true of the process of evolution itself, through which the genomes evolved—the ultimate source of the creativity we see in nature. Perhaps we identify in the genomes a delight in joking, in play, in senses such as vision, far in advance of what creatures need for mere survival. Perhaps from these we find in the process of evolution a constant urge to know its surroundings. Perhaps the ancient myth about humanity having fallen in love with the Earth and set out on a quest to discover it and merge with it was all along an intuition about evolution. Genomes, and the creatures they'd create, were all along a way for evolution to reach out and know the purely physical world.

STEP 27
Other ancient wisdoms

Ancient Roman thinking, like ours, had become
secular. Their old Olympian gods were long gone.
Emperors being made gods when they died was little
more than a fiction to maintain social order. The
Stoics' World Spirit might be invoked as part of
cosmic order but it involved no personal relationship.
Roman thinking was probably even more secular than
ours when we say "I'm not religious, but I am
spiritual." Educated Romans weren't even "spiritual."
In place of religion they practiced philosophies like
Stoicism.

Life was much tougher in Ancient times than it is
for us today so Romans looked to their philosophies,
or lifestyles, not so much for happiness, as we do, but
for ways to cope. When times were particularly
tough, and trouble unavoidable, the philosophy of
choice was Stoicism. To a Stoic, what mattered above
all was maintaining virtue, everything else—health,
wealth, even friends and family—were "indifferents."
Emotions were diseases of the mind that you
controlled through reason. Even happiness was an
indifferent. Only the satisfaction you got from
maintaining virtue was to be desired.

When times were less tough, the more appropriate
choice was Epicureanism. Epicureans preferred to
escape from Rome's turmoil into private retreats

where they could enjoy sophisticated pleasures in the company of a few friends. They looked down on simple bodily indulgences, such as drunkenness and gluttony, that were too soon satisfied. Instead they cultivated moderate and refined pleasures such as poetry and music that could be sustained indefinitely.

A third philosophy popular with the Romans was skepticism, the gleeful and skillful demolition of all principles believed in and promoted by others. The methods of classical skepticism played a large part in the development of modern science several centuries ago.

If after our abandonment of Christianity we reject physical determinism, ancient paganism can provide us with a rich bed of culture to revive and cultivate once more. Marcus Aurelius can provide us with a model for how to think about consciousness, for example.

Are we ready?

Playing catch up consciously

*If we're so wonderful,
why is our consciousness so primitive?
And what can we do about it?*

STEP 28
Consciousness, by comparison, so primitive

Compared to our wonderful bodies, which took hundreds of millions of years to evolve, our consciousness is still very primitive. Some authorities say it couldn't begin evolving until humans developed language perhaps only 50,000 years ago

Here's how I see that happening. I see consciousness beginning with the invention of "if." If you've probed into computer language you'll know that at the root of it are expressions like: "if such-and-such, then do one thing; else, do something else." "If... then..." implies it's possible to imagine alternative futures and judge between them.

Imagine being alive 50,000 years ago. Someone signs "antelope," points into the distance to the left, then points at you and to the right but then around to the left and signs "spear attack." Through signs you're being told, when an antelope shows up to the left, go around it and attack it from the rear. Then suppose the signs are repeated, but point in the opposite directions. You're being told, if an antelope shows up on the left, go to the right, if it shows up on the right, go to the left.

For you, that person would be astonishing. Even if they themselves aren't conscious of it, they can imagine alternative futures and think up appropriate responses. They can think "if... then..." What's more natural than that you, seeing them do it, assume you can too, and come up with the word "if." In other words, from someone else's behavior you can read that they have a mind in which they can suppose "if," and so you'll suppose you have a mind like that too. Once you make up and start using the word "if," and others copy you, they too will realize they have minds in which they can imagine alternative futures.

Then, if you've the right kind of brain, using the "if... then..." construction will induce consciousness in you.

We may never be able to define consciousness. It's unique, so there's nothing we can compare it to, to describe it. But here's my attempt: remember I supposed that all genomes shared the same consciousness. Think of that consciousness as being like a bank. For each of us the genomes set up an account in this bank, like theirs except we can't access any other account but our own. Once our brains set up their consciousness-accounts we become self-aware and have free will.

And able to learn a language. Modern languages come already equipped with all the "if," "else," "while," "until" functions a human consciousness needs for considering alternatives, and with the reason and logic we need for arriving at decisions.

We may have already begun to become conscious 50,000 years ago. But for how long have people had conscious experiences like ours? In his "The Origin of Consciousness in the Breakdown of the Bicameral

Mind" Julian Jaynes traced the emergence of consciousness in ancient writings. He found consciousness like ours missing from the Iliad but the beginnings of it present in the Odyssey. Say it emerged around 800 BC.

Recent milestones are the discoveries that we evolved, and of tools of self-awareness such as Freud's defense mechanisms. Freud's point was that we disguise our motivations from ourselves through processes of projection, repression, sublimation etc. Of course, once you learn about something like that it becomes part of self-awareness. That's one way consciousness advances.

If consciousness like ours emerged around 800 BC, that 50 lifetimes ago. How much can we expect to contribute to its further evolution in our own lifetime? Probably another 2%. Any ideas what those contributions might be?

STEP 29
Magic as legacy

Imagine getting used to talking about ourselves and the living creatures around us in terms of this new magic. We'd have one language—we could call that "scientism"—for talking about the non-living physical world—and another language, what I'll call "Intelligent Genie-ism," for talking about ourselves and other living creatures. We'd become, at least in the short term, dualists. We'd experience reality equally in both the intelligent-genome, conscious, way of thinking, and the scientific.

But deep down I'm not a dualist. I think our urge to discover will lead to a new study, possibly along the lines I suggested in my time travel story at the end of this book, by which we'll augment what we now call science and move to a new unified natural philosophy. I don't see dualism as a fundamental feature of reality, I think it signals a limitation in our thinking

As we go, new concepts and ways of thinking from this new discourse will migrate into everyday language and become a part of the mental apparatus our descendants inherit as they learn their mother tongue. That will be our primary contribution to the further evolution of our species.

To see where we are in the development of human

consciousness, I divide it into three stages.

First stage, from the invention of phonetic alphabets 3000 years ago up to around 200 AD. According to Julian Jaynes, consciousness like ours came into existence only when people could use phonetic alphabets to record their train of thought, and follow the trains of thought of other people, even after they were dead. Within only a few centuries Greek philosophy was in full swing. Meanings they created, such as Aristotle distinguishing between quality and quantity, bedded down as words in language we can all benefit from.

How much of modern consciousness did we get in stage one, from the Ancient Greeks and Romans? Are we much more civilized than they were? Did we need the Sermon on the Mount to become considerate of the meek, to learn to love one another? I don't think so. Here are some more extracts from Marcus Aurelius' meditations:

> A test: try living the life of a good man and see how it suits you—be the man happy with his fate, rejoicing in his acts of justice and bent on deeds of kindness…. Live in harmony with everything around you, and love—without reservations or conditions—those with whom you live and work. Let this be your one joy and delight: to go from one act of kindness to another with your mind fixed on God [the wisdom implicit in nature].

> There are three kinds of men in this world. The first, when he helps someone out, makes it known that he expects something in return. The

second would never be so bold, but in his mind he knows what he has done and considers the other person to be in his debt. The third somehow doesn't realize what he has done, but he's like a vine that bears fruit and asks for nothing more than the pleasure of producing grapes. A horse gallops, a dog hunts, a bee makes honey, one man helps another, and the vine bears fruit in due season.... Ask yourself— what could possibly please you more than to be great-souled, free, natural, gentle and devout?

Don't be a Caesar drunk with power and self-importance: it happens all to easily. Keep yourself simple, good, pure, sincere, natural, just, god-fearing, kind, affectionate, and devoted to your duty. Strive to be the man your training in philosophy prepared you to be. Fear God; serve mankind. Life is short; the only good fruit to be harvested in this earthly realm requires a pious disposition and charitable behavior.

Imagine what a thousand more years of development along these lines might not have accomplished! But **instead** people began agonizing as never before about meaning in life. The Roman Empire sank into the magics of Gnosticism, NeoPlatonism, and Christianity.

Stage two was Christendom. After a thousand years of it Spanish conquistadores would show no more consideration in their treatment of the Inca and Aztecs than the most brutal pagans. It would take another two centuries of immersion in the recovered writings of the Ancient World for later explorers like

Captain Cook to be more considerate and respectful towards the native people they met in new lands.

If we had continued the progress made from the composition of the Iliad up to the musings of the Emperor Marcus Aurelius for the even longer duration of the dominance of Christianity, I think we would have progressed further. I think we've little to lose by moving on from Christendom as if it never happened.

STEP 30
"Folk psychology" given its due

Two ideas are fundamental to this book. First, what matters most in life is conscious experience. Second, we can make our future conscious experiences richer by what we choose to be conscious of today.

But is that possible? Is being conscious something to find meaningful? And can we consciously choose what to conscious of? Is consciousness like that? Just what is it capable of? What's a good way to think about it?

Here's how I think about it—it may make no sense to you, it's just the best I can do. Imagine a flat sheet on which someone has sketched out everything that makes us tick: our cells, our muscles, our instincts, our senses, and so on. Altogether, a vast network of connections and intelligences. Before we became conscious, while we were still like other apes, other living creatures, that's all we were.

Then, starting at one point, a sort of glow appears. As languages develop and civilizations grow, that glow spreads. That glow is consciousness. It isn't something added, like a new organ, a brain or an elephant's trunk, it's just a subtle change in how things already are. The bigger that patch of glow, the more conscious we became. Consciousness wasn't a new thing, it was a condition that spread over what was already there.

Maybe it began with us becoming conscious of what we saw and heard. We weren't yet aware of what we were thinking, but once we said something or did something we became conscious of having said it or done it. Our saying and doing things began to glow, we became conscious of them. Who were we? We were what said those sayings and did those doings.

Why I find this idea useful is, what's aglow may be different in each of us. Human consciousness may not be something distinct, the same in every human being, but simply a distinctive glowing spread variously over what makes us tick, different from person to person.

Why this matters is, what matters to me about consciousness may mean nothing to you. Yet that's what this book is about. All this time you may have been thinking, "What's he talking about?" Now I have to lay my cards on the table. I have to tell you which part of all those connections and intelligences, that make up me, I experience being conscious of.

Fortunately, it's recently become easier to appreciate differences in how we experience consciousness. People with what's being called "aphantasia" are discovering each other and making the condition better known. They refer to themselves as "aphants." If you're an aphant, when you close your eyes you can't visualize anything. At aphantasia.com it's described as being unable to visualize in the mind's eye, hear sound in the mind's ear, or imagine sensory experiences, outside the present moment. That is, as it actually happens.

What causes this? Is it something wrong with these people's brains? No. Their vision and visual memory are working fine. They can describe in words how things look, and when they open their eyes they can recognize things. They just can't consciously bring anything visual to mind, they can't imagine it. In my terms, for them the "glow" of consciousness doesn't extend over visual memory and imagination. They can do anything as well as anyone. Being an aphant didn't stop the writer Oliver Sachs from being as wise and informed about consciousness as anyone else alive.

In a video on youtube.com (search for "My Girlfriend Has No Inner Monologue") the boyfriend says to his girlfriend, "You function as complexly in society as I do, even more efficiently than I do," She nods. Then to us he says, "When she closes her eyes there's no internal dialog, no words, no images, nothing. She can have a complex thought without any problem, without using language to do it. She just knows it."

She tells us, "It's completely silent in my head, I've no interior dialog. I can think a sentence but it doesn't naturally happen, I just know everything, in an abstract kind of way, without having to be conscious of it. I can't imagine doing things consciously. It's like, my body needs to do something—it's done." I think for her my wanting to enrich consciousness couldn't make sense. Enrich what? Choose what to be conscious of? How? Change what she'd be conscious of in the future? She'll be no more conscious in the future than she is now.

Absence of mind's eye occurs in only about 2-3% of people, but it's particularly common among scientists. Scientists with aphantasia will experience their brains making all their decisions for them without them being conscious of it. They'll experience the world being just as physical determinism says it is, with no role for consciousness.

Is this where the idea of physical determinism comes from? I asked one promoter of physical determinism if he experienced consciousness and, after a pause, he admitted he didn't. This could have been true for Gilbert Ryle whose 1949 book "Mind" started the modern enthusiasm for physical determinism. Contemporaries of his noted that he appeared to have very little inner life. For people like that, other people's claim of having free will can only seem to be a delusion. This may explain why physical determinism is so popular in the sciences.

And, more practically, it may explain why science's theory of evolution, which takes no account of consciousness, is the only account permitted in the school science classroom. Personally, I think that amounts to promotion of a particular cognitive style and should have no place in science. What the rest of us experience, being able to arrive at decisions consciously, some scientists call "folk psychology," as if compared to them we're all unthinking primitives. I find that offensive, don't you?

I do have mind's eye. I experience being aware of my thoughts as I have them, while I'm gazing onto an imaginary sketch pad held in front of me. On this sketchpad I can project images, draw sketches, imagine paintings, compose text. I can bring to mind other people's voices, music, though faintly. I can manipulate people faces and voices as a puppeteer can, and with my hand sketch what I'm imagining. The imagined graphics aren't as vibrant as what I actually see with my eyes open, they're more like after-images. I can experience them even when my eyes are open. It's as if the outside world and the mind's eye are on separate layers, I can be conscious of both, they're equally real, equally demanding to be accounted for.

And free will? I experience being able to consciously decide what to think about, project images and words onto the mind's eye's sketch pad, and arrange and re-arrange my thoughts there. On the other hand, in my few attempt to meditate I could deliberately empty my mind's eye, monitor new thoughts popping up and consciously banish them. I experience being in control in my conscious experiences.

How about the richness of conscious experience? For me various kinds of conscious experiences feel different. I experience some as being more intense, more enjoyable, more complex than others. I can imagine them being made even richer. For example, if I thought knowing more about architecture would make my conscious experiences richer I might consciously direct my body to order a book on it online. I experience communications going both ways between consciousness and brain and body. There's no aspect of conscious experience I can't talk or write about, for example. My brain has access to all of that, and that includes all the decisions I arrive at in consciousness, as I think them. My brain could easily be taking them as orders to be given physical expression.

So do we have free will or not? For me the question should be retired. One kind of consciousness implies we don't, another kind implies we do. One justifies belief in physical determinism, the other justifies belief in consciousness and free will being real, as real as physical matter, and possibly involved in how we evolved. The natural philosophy you settle on is going to support how you experience the world.

How can the experience of consciousness differ so much from person to person, so much more than our bodies vary from person to person? I believe, because consciousness evolved so recently. It hasn't had time to become the same everywhere.

I've already introduced Julian Jaynes. He supposed that consciousness first emerged among the rulers of great cities that came into existence only 5000 years ago.

Two thousand years later the first syllabic alphabets appeared and let you record whatever you were thinking as if you were saying it. Now any thought you had and recorded in writing could induce conscious experiences in someone else as they read it.

Something like this happened in many parts of the world as around the same time, and in each case a distinctive pattern of consciousness threaded its way over mind and body. This would assume one shape in China, another in India, another among the Israelites, another among the Greeks. All became conscious, all could translate from their language into the others, but each came with distinctive conscious experiences depending on which parts of body and mind their consciousness threaded its way across.

I believe this is still true. I believe the reach of consciousness in each of us is affected by where we were born, what languages we speak, what religious tradition we were brought up in, what kind of education we had, and the impact on us of particularly intense experiences

Finally, one last difference among us—our attitudes towards consciousness. For my two most resolute critics, consciousness is not something to question and mess around with, in its way it's sacred, better left alone. By contrast, for me, consciousness invites tinkering, like a camera that I'm free to take apart and experiment with. The 3D photography I practiced as a child involved me treating my eyes simply as optical instruments. That attitude has stayed with me all my life. I'm always looking for new ways to enrich consciousness, beyond how it "naturally" comes.

This idea of extending consciousness by embracing new tools, does it appeal to you? Here's a chance to find out. When I came across Freud's ego defenses, or defense mechanisms, they made a big impression on me. They're ways unconscious parts of our minds protect the conscious parts from what they'd find disagreeable:

Repression—disagreeable thoughts are kept away from consciousness.

Denial—facts we'd be upset by are denied access to consciousness.

Projection—what we don't want to acknowledge about ourselves gets attributed to others.

Displacement—dangerous impulses are redirected onto innocuous objects.

Freud regarded these as unconscious defenses. But of course, once you come across them you have an opportunity to make them part of consciousness, and that's what I chose to do. They've become part of a meta-consciousness—a conscious and internal monitoring of consciousness itself.

Does that appeal to you? Then, let's proceed.

But first, a warning.

STEP 31

A collapse of consciousness. A story.

Of course, progress in consciousness isn't inevitable? History's proved that over and over again. Suppose we all turn away from this challenge of applying ourselves to the advance of consciousness, and just let things drift as we're doing today. What may happen?

Here's a cautionary tale.

Collapse

We are sitting in a theatre, in the far distant future, watching a troupe of acrobats perform their version of the history of our time. The lights dim. A figure prances on stage.

On each shoulder our dancer wears a stuffed bluebird. He continues to dance around the stage, as if entranced. He reaches out in front of him, dances with invisible partners, and hums, as if listening to music.

He is acting out the famous "bluebird" advertisement for the virtual reality headset that set the tone of the final fifty years of the Modern Age. The original Modern-World ad, now being displayed in the background, showed a youth smiling, enthralled, with a bluebird on each shoulder. Each bird holds a semitransparent wing over one of the youth's eyes, while it whispers in his ear. The ad was for a helmet that picked up signals from satellites and projected them before you as a virtual impression of real dramatic action, through a mix of stereophonic sound and 3D moving pictures. The result was a convincing picture of another world. Yet, because the visor was semitransparent, the viewer could see through it, to carry on his real life. The effect was as if he were living in two "real" worlds at once.

This technological marvel rose to dominate the world's attention through a series of related discoveries. First, a computer program called "Thespia" was invented, which could, in seconds, generate synthetic actors and their speech, mathematically—computed talking and acting figures that appeared to be real but whose behavior was controlled by software. At the rear of the stage we see what he is seeing, acted by some of the students. They enjoy playing these computed actors, first stiffly and jerkily, then with increasing deftness as the software improves. Initially, the computer's dramas employ modern-world schemes of motivation and action development, ranging from old-fashioned melodrama to psychoanalysis.

The helmets are a massive success. For a people already addicted to drama, watching it for some six hours a day, the new helmet makes drama available continuously, while you maintain, as best you can, the rest of your normal activities. Since these dramas cost little to produce—the software can generate them for next to nothing—the airwaves are soon full of rival broadcasting stations.

The next development is to make the helmets

interactive. They now tell the broadcaster which channel is being watched, and at what point in the action the wearer turns to see something else. With this feedback, the broadcasters can experiment to see what people most want to see. At this point, one station tried a very curious experiment: random dramatic development. The computers are set to generate action using AI, without any guiding principle, at the same time analyzing people's response, to detect patterns of interest. This new program is wildly successful, and much copied. The number of headsets soars into the billions, and the phenomenon spreads across the globe, as the computers translate their synthetic action into more and more languages.

A frantic race now develops to use the feedback to extract new principles of dramatic organization. In a few years, all the old patterns of plot development are made obsolete by new patterns. In a giddy convergence, one new principle emerges as the winner, and will remain dominant for the remainder of the Modern World.

The new principle is called "tradition programming," but we could better name it "tradition unraveling." Analysis of random programming reveals that, for most people, the greatest dramatic excitement of all comes from their own traditions being split back into their components. And that this is most effectively achieved if the traditions are unraveled systematically from the loose, most recent, end, in the reverse order they were created. What this means is that the fuel for this new medium is the chains of traditions evolved over thousands and thousands of years.

"Tradition studies" become the leading edge of commerce, and large research teams study history and trace chains of such traditions as "royalty" and "patriotism," which are then fed into the computers for unraveling in drama. It's like the consumption centuries earlier by artists, using perspective, of the prior reverence for sacred scenes, except that now it takes place in minutes instead of decades. An intensive analysis of world culture follows, and more and more themes are settled on for unraveling, such as "responsibility," "democracy," and "pity," different for each nation but subject everywhere to the thrill of tradition-unraveling. As the audience becomes habituated to this new thrill, the speed of corruption of the traditions has to increase, to maintain people's attention, and meanings more central to the core of sensation have to be exploited. Restraints on violating physical and sexual taboos had already evaporated in early modern times; remaining meanings relating of authority and altruism are quickly exhausted. The search inevitably turns to the self itself, and its underpinnings. The broadcasters, engaged in brutal competition for the audience, have no option but to turn to the unraveling of the structure of the self.

As a result, the self takes center stage once more, and is poked and prodded to distinguish its compartments and its qualities. Language is devised to describe it, AI begins to unravel it. At this point fierce reaction develops. The program of tradition-unraveling had been no secret and had been tolerated as just one more legitimate extension of entertainment. But a serious attempt to dismantle the self is another matter, and generates tremendous opposition, particularly since, in most cultures, the self has to a great extent been formed by religion which still remains a strong force.

The battle over the self involves the entire world. The broadcast industry is run from only a few nations, but their satellites are busy night and day, broadcasting to any country with a big-enough audience. These countries now fight back to preserve their traditional sense of self. For five years the issue is undecided, and it seems that the reaction, led by a China on the point of assuming world leadership, will win. But the broadcast industry is by far the world's biggest, and appetite for the new drama is too strong, and in the end the broadcasters win. Grimly they set themselves to grind away the remaining fictions supporting the self, while China licks its wounds and waits for a second chance that will never come.

While we've been concerned with this story, the stage has filled with helmeted dancers gathering to celebrate advances in the new medium. To celebrate the linking of the world's nations in a single broadcast unity, the dancers begin to climb on one another's shoulders, forming the wall the school's performance is famous for. Younger acrobats climb up the wall of bodies to take their places higher up.

The last member of the team of acrobats climbs to take her position at the top of the wall, and the whole wall of helmeted acrobats begins to sway, to sway. Seemingly unaware of their danger, the acrobats gaze vacantly ahead, rapt in attention to their helmets. The swaying increases, and increases, until with a crash the whole wall collapses, and the acrobats all separately tumble to the ground, and lie still. In one moment, the modern world is no more.

STEP 32
Consciousness enriched

The way technology is going, that could easily happen.

But we don't have to go along. We could resolve to be more conscious of being conscious, and make it magnificent.

What would such a magnificent consciousness feel like? I can't imagine. We won't know until we achieve it. And to achieve it we first have to believe it's possible. To do that we have to banish the scientific origin theory that tells us we're nothing more than the product of a crude physical process, and that there's nothing wonderful about us at all. The way I see it, Darwinism and the modern synthesis have acted as nothing more than blinkers concealing from us what we needed to know.

What I'm saying we need to know now is, there's a capacity for magnificence evolved into each one of us.

Is that really true? Are we really all that wonderful? Compared to insects, that look so wonderfully complex from the outside, we don't look very wonderful. Besides a lot of skin and a little hair there's not much to see from the outside, except our eyes. So let's see how wonderful they are, and assume that everything else about us is as wonderful as that. What we want to find out is, are we as wonderfully equipped as we'll need to be for our conscious experiences to become wonderful too?

How wonderful is the eye? Mostly it's filled with a kind of jelly and light goes straight through it. For light to form an image at the back of an eye it gets bent twice, once at the cornea at the front of the eye, and again by a lens inside the eye. Amazingly, although all this is living tissue it's transparent. Then, although images made by a glass lens have colored fringes, the lens in an eye, by growing more dense in the center, forms images without colored fringes, they're sharp. The lens grows as we age but as it grows it becomes less dense in the center so the image it forms stays sharp. The body constantly replaces most of the chemicals it consists of and the cornea, which does most of the bending of light, gets replaced every few days yet, again, our vision stays sharp. This is all wonderful.

But even more amazing are fine muscles that run from the rim of the lens to the inside surface of the eye. By the tightening and relaxing of these muscles the lens becomes more bunched up or flatter, changing how close or far away the lens focuses. And what I find most wonderful of all is, they fall in with our conscious intentions. As we consciously shift our attention from one object to another, these muscles tighten or relax, bringing what we're paying attention to into sharp focus. Something physical in our bodies—these fine muscles—all the time track and respond to what we consciously choose to make ourselves aware of. The processes of evolution have equipped us with bodies responsive to what we make ourselves conscious of. Free will results from this fusion of body and mind.

This response of the muscles around the lens of the eye to our conscious attention illustrates an important principle of the new wisdom—the processes of evolution "know about" consciousness. We see that in how these muscles respond as we consciously choose what to look at, moment by moment, focusing close, then focusing at a distance as we redirect our attention.

Here's a glance back at the path we've taken. I started out looking for new meaning in life. I found it in the prospect of all our future conscious experiences, particularly as we could enrich them by what we choose to be conscious of today. At once I ran up against physical determinism. Claiming to speak for modern science it said everything about us, now and in the future, was already determined by the laws of physics, it wasn't up to us to choose what to be conscious of. Turned out, physical determinism wasn't science at all, it was an ancient magic once again pretending to be science, this time claiming to account for how we evolved through a purely physical mechanism, Charles Darwin's "natural selection."

Wasn't there a corresponding magic that opposed determinism, I asked myself, that we could reconnect with and update? I found that in Charles' grandfather's "living filament." In this living filament I found an entirely different picture of how the world is put together—including a new agent that drove evolution, that like us was intelligent, conscious and creative.

Remember those flat disks in insect larvae, how concealed in them were the legs and wings they'd become when you pulled them out from the center? For me, like that, concealed in the ideas of Erasmus Darwin was how wonderful we'd actually evolved to be. But because that was hard to account for with a reductionist explanation, that wisdom has lain untapped for two centuries, in favor of purely physical and chemical theories.

It's time to take play catch-up. And put our new wisdom into practice.

Magic in practice

*In this Section I try out
various ways we can apply our
new magic, along with the rest of our
accumulated wisdom.*

STEP 33

The self we come with.

"You," said the caterpillar. "Who are you?"

Alice said she wasn't sure.

I think she speaks for many of us. Who, or what, are we? Before we set out to find new meaning in life, let's look at the assumption about ourselves we already come with, that we might want to tackle first.

Who or what are we?

Our bodies are physical. We know what purely physical things are like. But we're more than that. What else are we?

Another part comes from being a living creature, an alive human being. What that means is, we're the kind of creature our genome specifies.

And there's culture—language, education, our personal experiences, and so on.

And... Isn't there more? Not a soul exactly, but something like that? Something spiritual? Something that let's us tune into energy currents running through the universe? A higher being?

I don't think so. I think we have to find all that in what we've already covered—our physical bodies, our genome, our culture. If they don't seem enough, perhaps we've been underestimating them.

Our bodies are more wonderful than we usually

realize, as I've already pointed out at great length. They may contribute more to consciousness than we usually give them credit. Every so often I run a test to see if my brain will give me (my consciousness) access to the maps it uses to run me. Will my brain give my consciousness access to the maps it uses to identify the nerves and ligaments controlling the hand, for example—can I consciously bend the last joint of the ring finger of my right hand, something I don't think I'd ever tried to do before? No problem. Bending the second joint I could do at once, bending the final joint took a little bit more concentration, but yes, without knowing how, my "will" was able to thread its way using my body's map of the nerves and muscles to control just that joint. Brain, body and conscious mind work together like buddies.

And culture of course is wonderful, our languages for example giving us a vast body of meanings to draw from. And our genome? It's from there that all the other wonders come. That's what makes our bodies so wonderful, what equipped us in the first place to create culture. So everything that's wonderful about us, I've concluded, comes from the genome, soul and all.

Why don't we already know that? Because we've been wearing blinders. Something's been hiding from us how wonderful evolution has made us.

Once again, the villain is that apostle of determinism, Charles Darwin.

During Darwin's lifetime, you practiced science by turning everything into atoms. Darwin did this with evolution. Built into his theory of natural selection is the assumption that the individuals in a species come basically all the same, like atoms, blanks ready for attaching another set of atoms to— characteristics. What got tested for fitness and passed on from one generation to the next was these characteristics, that the environment could select for, separately, one by one.

We've since discovered he was wrong. The unit of inheritance isn't individual characteristics. What gets passed on from one generation to the next is genes, and genes don't correspond to individual characteristics one to one. What individuals pass on from one generation to another is not different values for individual characteristics but our genomes as a whole.

We know that now, but the damage has been done. In accepting Darwin's account of how we evolved we've unconsciously accepted those same assumptions, that we're basically all the same, differing only in the value of a limited number of characteristics like IQ and eye color.

I'm dragging you straight into an old battle, between nature and nurture. When people pictured the genome as simple set of scripts and switches, they couldn't imagine how it could code for all the power and subtlety of human culture and creativity. But now we know it can. Behind every genius throughout history there's been a set of chromosomes as complex and unique as each of us carries, in every cell of our body.

Each of us is wonderful, just the way we come. We can start feeling wonderful by simply assuming we are, that our genome makes us that way.

Let's find ways that can lead us to new meaning in life.

STEP 34
Integrity

Remember the second principle of my new magic? We can enrich our future conscious experiences by what we choose to make ourselves conscious of today. How would we do that? And what effect will doing it have on us, as we go along? What kind of person will we turn into?

How I see us doing that is, by managing our meanings, both those built into us by evolution, and those we pick up as we go along. This will be partly an individual matter, because our genomes are individual, different for each of us. We'll have to learn how as we go—as our conscious experiences fail to satisfy us as much as we expected we'll have to adjust our goals. The task facing each child will be to predict what will most satisfy his or her future self, a task that will continue throughout life, with the payoff of ever-richer conscious experiences.

What is this practice likely to do to us? I think it will lead to—and here I'm going to use an old fashioned word—integrity. But I'm going to give that word a new meaning. Instead of integrity meaning how consistent and reliable we seem to other people, I'll use it to mean how we'll come to seem to ourselves as we manage the meanings available to us. That process of choosing what to be conscious of so as to enrich our future experiences will become a form of life-long self education.

Now I'm no model for anything, but here are two ways I try to shape my integrity. If a drama has someone being killed, or even someone drawing a weapon with intent to kill, I stop watching. Killing as entertainment I experience as damaging to what I'm calling my integrity. Another example: I shield my attention from advertising, not because it's less important than what I want to look at but so my attention can experience following a coherent path, not continually diverted from that path by something else.

This must sound to you a very stern notion of what life is about. But I think we owe it to ourselves to monitor what claims our attention, for how it could affect our future experiences. According to a Wall Street Journal/NBC News poll in 2019, 82% of Americans thought social media a waste of time compared to only 15% who think those media help us use our time well. That's almost six times as many people feeling social media are a waste of time. My new magic may prompt you to ask yourself of any social media, is devoting attention to it the best way to enrich my future conscious experiences?

Aren't our remaining conscious experiences worth making an investment in today?

STEP 35
Notes from a not very magical life

You weren't brought up with the finest Greek and Roman scholars as your tutors as Marcus Aurelius was, you weren't trained from an early age to be emperor of Rome. So you may think it's too late now to start developing a new set of mental habits.

Here's what our emperor said about that. "Think of yourself as dead. You have lived your life. Now take what's left and live it properly." What's left? And how can you live it properly? What does it mean in our place and time to live properly? Perhaps it means consciously deciding what habits we'd need to develop so as to enrich the conscious experiences left to us, and resolving to do and think what it takes to acquire those habits. Or, in my terms, developing personal integrity. That makes what we choose to think about today very significant.

I can't say I pay much conscious attention to it. But I do seem quite naturally to take it into account. I took up drawing in my 40s, doggedly tracing over magazine illustrations hour after hour to train my hand. It worked. After a few years of this I could draw quite well. I suppose I enjoyed that dogged practice a bit, but mainly I did it for how I anticipated I'd enjoy drawing when I'd finished. Recently I've been trying to learn Latin, so in the future I'll be able to think the way the Ancient Romans did, with the verb coming last in each sentence. That's an investment in future conscious experiences. It's a principle we probably all subscribe to, naturally. But it may be worth giving more conscious thought to. What senses are the last to go, as we age? Perhaps in our senior years it would be wise to develop refinement in use of just those senses.

What else can developing what I'm calling integrity give us? I think, greater self-respect. I feel I do gain self-respect from reflecting on how I embody the towering power of evolution. I feel comforted by knowing the genome in each cell of my body carries all the information needed for making a complete human being, and still carries wisdom I've not yet accessed.

One key to gaining this kind of self-respect, for me, is learning more about myself and other evolved creatures. How wonderful has evolution made me? How amazing is the organization of my body? A good read here is William Paley's "Natural Theology." He's another of those British enlightenment figures whose intellects had not yet been cramped by scientific specialization. Read the middle half, which is about the wonders of the human body. For an up-to-date account purchase "The Complete Human Body."

Experiencing the wonderfulness of nature is as simple as entering a garden and meditating on any one plant, seeing how it grows. It's helpful to know some of the details, knowing that the leaves it spreads to catch sunlight are filled with chloroplasts carrying out strings of elaborate processes to turn that energy into chemical energy, for further growth. I have three textbooks at home on botany, three on insects, two on birds. Watch a bird sitting on a telephone wire, suddenly it flips around and is facing the other way. It happens faster than our eyes can take in. Imagine what that must take, what muscles must be involved. Is it using its wings to swing itself around?

We are as wonderful, as nature made us, as these creatures are. To embark on enriching our future conscious experiences we must feel that wonderfulness, and want to make it true of our consciousness as well.

Every so often, in the past, I'd struggle to appreciate something, like poetry or certain artists like Cezanne, only to realize I hadn't come equipped to appreciate it. I've come to trust my gut feeling about such things. I've come to rely on ways I react to things, naturally. I've come to see it's up to each of us, individually, to come to terms with limitations in how we come equipped, while at the same celebrating what's particularly wonderful in us, perhaps something that no one ever before has discovered in themselves.

I know I must sound as if I'm encouraging extreme individualism. But I cringe at that. It reminds me of Hitler's "Thinking with the blood," and you know what that lead to. We may know we're wonderful, but then so is everyone else. There's nothing special about us for being wonderful. It comes with being human.

STEP 36
Interpersonal practice

For a Christian, other people deserve respect because they are just as wonderfully fashioned by God and just as precious to Him as you are yourself. But once you cease to be a Christian, what then? Why respect others to any degree at all? What is there to celebrate about someone else when they're just as determined in what they think and do as a rock falling off a cliff and spitting into smaller fragments. It's all just physics.

No, it's even worse than that, wrote the French philosopher Sartre: Hell is other people.

We get the opposite opinion from the Ancient World, from the Greek philosopher Epicurus. Epicurus found in other people the opportunity to make friends, and for him friends were one of the greatest sources of enduring pleasure. To be a friend, he said, you must indulge and focus on the other person at least as much as you indulge and focus on yourself. In my terms, you must find—and show you find—other people as wonderful as you know you are.

When you look someone in the eye, recall that that eye is just as complex and wonderful as either of yours. In that eye, the other person possesses an optical instrument much more capable than anything modern technology can fashion. And they'll probably have two such eyes, information from them differing ever so slightly, from which their brain can register depth perception. Keep looking into those eyes. The other person's magnificence is most clearly sensed there.

Then recall that, highly evolved though your eyes may be, both of you are at a very early stage in the development of consciousness. A visitor from the remote future would find the conscious experiences of both of you very primitive indeed. To such a visitor, there'd be nothing significant to recommend one of you over the other. What to do?

I have a radical suggestion—say nothing. Look for ways to engage the right sides of your brains, the more intuitive and creative sides, home of music and poetry. The right brain is much older and wiser than the left. Try communicating in song, hold each other's left hands (more right-brain), flip through tarot cards. Speak as Quakers speak at their meetings: only as moved to, not out of obligation.

Aim to become an appreciative visitor in the other person's mental landscape. Relish it as you would a visit to an exotic locale in a strange land. That is what it will most likely resemble. True, it is a courtesy to make oneself knowable, but it is as great a courtesy to make an effort to know the other person.

STEP 37

Society

I think it's hard to develop a new lifestyle alone.
Could we create a group practice for this new magic?

I can imagine congregations gathering weekly to
celebrate their new natural philosophy. There would
be readings from the great naturalists such as
Aristotle and Charles Darwin, and ancient texts from
throughout the world. Illustrated talks would detail
the marvels of animal and human physiology. People
might testify to discoveries they'd made about their
own genetic dispositions. There'd be singing to help
us share our common civilized humanity.

Between these gatherings, smaller groups might
meet for "Difference talk." That's a way people who
start out disagreeing about something can resolve that
disagreement by having a conversation about it. In the
course of this conversation you discard everything
you agree about, focusing only on your
disagreements. You pursue them deeper, level by
level, until you reach generic dispositions that lie at
their root, that you can understand account for your
original disagreement. It's a way for people to plumb
the depths of their own and each other's meanings.

I'd like recognition of genetic difference to be
extended to philosophy. Maybe each philosophy
should be seen as the outlook of a particular genetic

disposition rather than as a comment on the human condition in general. Alternative philosophies would not then be seen as errors to be corrected but as renderings of differing genetic bases for thought and experience.

STEP 38
Where real progress lies

You want progress? It's offered us on every side. Smarter phones, virtual reality goggles, self-driving cars, DNA analysis, life extension. We're urged to hop aboard this historical movement that's all the time being upgraded with wonderful new toys and tricks. Wherever it's headed, it's taking us there faster and faster. Implied is, unless we go faster and faster, we'll never get there.

But where is "there"? Just possibly there isn't any "there" there. World population is forecast to plateau within a few decades. Our grandchildren may find themselves part of a shrinking population, in a shrinking economy, less concerned with new technologies to keep it growing than in finding alternative sources of meaning. In themselves, perhaps. In what makes creatures like them evolve. They may find new wisdom in the old saying, wherever you go, there you are. Maybe that's a good place to head for. Maybe that's where we should be heading, right now.

Suppose, just suppose, we stopped spending on consumer "goods." That spending accounts for 70% of the US economy, I've read. What would an economy based on other kinds of goods be like? A lot of people are thinking about that. One idea is, give everyone a small wage, just enough to keep body and soul together. But if no one works, what does the economy consist of? I take seriously that any proposal for a new way to live has to support some kind of an economy. Does my magic come with the makings of a new kind of economy?

Turns out, economies depend on something being of value. And values are basically meanings. Gold can only support an economy if we define it as having value. So we could simply come up with new values. Here's one—wanting our surroundings to be beautiful. Here's another—demolish all unused buildings. That will become big business once population begins to shrink.

Bigger than that, though, is putting a price on ways each of us is wonderful. That idea is so far out I can't imagine what it'd be like. But that's the logic built into the new magic. As we get to know ourselves better we'll find within us new meanings, new values, to make an economy out of, that are likely to satisfy us far more than today's manufactured goods.

New values, not new technologies, will power the economies of the future.

Ultimate meanings

*I know that by being as speculative
as I am in this Section I may discredit
all the Steps I've already made.
But how should a book on meaning
in life end except with some wild
blue-sky visions of the future?*

STEP 39
We have to make it up

Why did we evolve to become so exceptional?
Simultaneously we evolved to walk upright, our front
legs freed to become hands so we can make tools and
art and manage fire. We became able to form words
and make up and learn languages. We became smart
enough to create civilization. We became conscious,
we can say what bothers us, and look for meaning.

What does all that evolving, in just a few million
years—much of it in the last few hundred thousand—
say about our relationship to genomes, and the world?

Here's one possible answer: Four billion years
ago, when the genomes first became conscious, they
had to cope with a constant barrage of catastrophes.
Meteor strikes, volcanoes, earthquakes; the Earth's
crust was fractured and driven this way and that.
These were the genomes' heroic days. In the face of
this barrage they developed their particular genius for
creating life, in all its magnificent variety.

The rain of catastrophes gradually lessened but
still, seven eighths of the way to the present, the Earth
grew a coat of ice a mile think, and almost all life
died. Afterwards, the genomes exulted in having an
almost clean slate on which to map out even more
miraculous creatures. Again, a couple of hundred
thousand years later, vast volcanic eruptions culled

almost all life, and the genomes exulted once more in the unfettered exercise of their powers.

But the rain of catastrophes continued to lessen. The genomes began to yearn for a return to the heroic days of evolving in the face of constant catastrophes.

So they created us.

This is a very comforting vision of our destiny because we're already well on our way to achieving it. All we need do is go on creating catastrophes as we are.

But it's only one possible vision among many. Can we come up with something more inspiring?

How about this? What's special about the particular gifts the genomes gave us—our smarts, hands and language? They equipped us to create civilization. Along with civilization came science and technology. Our mission is to use our technology to travel to other planets, carrying the genomes with us, throughout the solar system and beyond. That's what they created us for.

This vision is more challenging. But it's hard for us, individually, to achieve any part of this vision, unless like Elon Musk we plan to send spaceships to Mars. Let's come up with something we can each participate in.

Remember me pointing out how genomes could evolve new species of living creatures. They could do this simply by bringing an existing species to mind and thinking changes into its genes.

Now let's project that back onto ourselves. Why

did the genomes give us minds like theirs where thoughts could evolve? What lead them to make us in their own image?

When did the genomes invent dreaming? They invented it long before we came along. Our pets, for example, we can see their whiskers and paws twitch as they sleep. They're dreaming. Why? It isn't essential for life, not all creatures seem to dream.

Like our pets we dream too. And when we wake after dreaming, we remember having been conscious while we dreamed. Could that be what consciousness was originally created for?

Time for some more magical thinking. Are you ready?

After a meteorite killed off the ground-dwelling dinosaurs, the genomes once again took the opportunity to embed, in living creatures, entirely new features. Into certain mammals they built a new and much more rapid way the genomes could communicate with one another—consciousness. Into these mammals they built consciousness in the form of dreaming during sleep. Through this medium of mammals dreaming the genomes could communicate with one another much faster than before.

That's what they invented dreaming for!

Then they came up with a new idea—could they take a creature conscious like that and equip it with advanced mental skills, such as creativity and reason, complex enough for thoughts to evolve within it? Could they equip it to think for itself, as they themselves did? Then, since thoughts could evolve much faster than DNA molecules could, genome intelligences could migrate from those DNA molecules to brains and evolve there at lightning speed.

For their test creature they settled on a line of apes, and created us. They made us able to be conscious while we're awake. And to be conscious, and creative.

In this vision, our mission is to prepare ourselves to become the next platform for the process of evolution. Our destiny is, through perfecting the apparatus of consciousness, through our thoughts evolving, to become the leading edge of evolution.

The fact that I can come up with three visions shows how arbitrary such visions are. They're just the creation of a moment. Next week I might come up with three more. But since my magic would be incomplete without any vision at all I've had to settle on one, as the official vision. I settled on that last one. Of the three visions it's the most speculative and least plausible but it accounts for something that cries out to be explained—why we dream, and why in dreaming we're conscious?

And, it provides each of us with a role in the further evolution of our species: through the study of nature within us and without we can learn about our own personal genome and use that to shape our conscious experiences around, so the intelligence of that genome can escape its genetic form and migrate into human minds!

So my ultimate phantasy vision is, we evolve to

become the primary platform for the further progress of evolution. We begin by making our conscious experiences as wonderful as our bodies have evolved to be, as wonderful as our eyes are.

OK, I'm done. The rest is up to you.

STEP 40
"Time travel through the evolution revolution"

Here's a fiction in which I imagine a future science through which we humans tap into the wisdom of evolution. This story first appeared in my previous book, "Re-thinking What it Means We Evolved."

Four hundred years ago new discoveries plunged us into the scientific revolution. Two hundred years ago we made another major discovery—we evolved. Why hasn't that led to another revolution?

I'm a writer. I don't have to wait until a revolution happens, I can take us there right now. I flag down a passing time machine promising "Evolution Revolution Tours." It glides to a halt, the doors open, we step inside. "Jane at your service," says a cheerful young woman at the controls.

OK, I say, let's be on our way.

Jane's hands flutter over the controls. There's a brief shudder. "That was it," she says, "the revolution, we're on the other side." She turns to face us. "Now, what would you like to know?

"Where are we going?" I ask.

"We're going to touch down three times," she says, "to see how differently the revolution made people think about what it meant they evolved."

"How does time travel work?" I ask.

"The same way history does" she says. "It gets its power from new ideas. To get us to our first landfall we'll be traversing four ideas laid end to end."

Once you're under way, time travel is pretty boring. There's nothing to look at. "Tell me about these ideas," I say. She picks them off on her fingers.

"Idea Number One: Reality includes non-physical processes

"Conscious experiences don't have weight or location. You can't sort them and put them in boxes. They aren't physical. But we all have them. So here's something that's part of our everyday reality, that's non-physical. Let's check—if you experience conscious experiences as part of everyday reality, raise your hand."

I raise my hand.

"You raised your hand, so you're revolution-ready. What made you raise your hand was something only your consciousness could know—that you experience having conscious experiences. What's revolutionary is realizing that conscious experiences—thinking or feeling or experiencing something—while they're not physical, can make something physical happen, like make you raise your hand. Brains that are physical and consciousnesses that are non-physical can tell each other what to do. They can work together.

"So Idea Number One is: Physical processes in brains can interact with non-physical processes in consciousness. We need that idea to connect us to Idea Number Two.

"Idea Number Two: Non-physical processes can be accessed through mind

"Those non-physical processes of consciousness, let's call where they operate, 'mind.' But instead of thinking of it as a place, think of it more as a banking system where, instead of an account giving you access to money, it gives you access to non-physical processes like those in consciousness.

"How do you set up an account in this 'mind'? You don't. Your brain does it for you. The way the human brain evolved it can plug in and set up an account for you, automatically. Then you're conscious. It's as easy as that. You didn't ask to become conscious, it just happened, right?

"Idea Number Two is: By setting up accounts in mind that provide access to non-physical processes, brains can establish conscious selves. We need that idea to engage with Idea Number Three.

"Idea Number Three: The genome is a brain

"The genome is a genetic blueprint. It's all the specifications for a living creature. In us it's written as a few dozen molecules, called chromosomes, that we've a copy of in the nucleus of every cell in our bodies. But, rather than thinking of the genome as molecules think of it instead as 'one long string of genetic code' that carries a lot of information.

"Here's something else about it that's extraordinary. It's alive—it's part of a living creature—but while individual living creatures die, the genome lives on, because it's copied from each generation to the next. It's the only part of living creatures that's existed ever since life first began. And here's something else about it that's amazing: As creatures evolved to become more complex the genome has grown longer, able to hold more information.

"So, does that qualify the genome to be a brain? It may not appear to be as complex as our brains but it's been evolving for 1000 times as long. And it holds a mind-boggling amount of information. There's nothing else on Earth remotely like it.

"So Idea Number Three is: For all intents and purposes the genome is a brain."

Jane turns back to the dashboard and fiddles with some controls. "To maintain our speed of travel," Jane says, "we have to join Ideas Two and Three. Like this:

"Idea Number Four: An entirely new mechanism of evolution

"Remember how I supposed brains, by opening accounts for us in mind, can make us conscious. If the genome is a brain and if it can open accounts for itself in consciousness too, who or what is it that becomes conscious?

"Whatever it is, could that be what drives evolution? I'll show you why it could.

"If the genome can become conscious then presumably it can think. What happens then? Well, what happens when we think? When we think we make changes to our brains. Take memory for example. To be sure of remembering something you can deliberately, consciously, think it to yourself several times over to make sure it gets imprinted in your brain. What you're doing is consciously etching a physical change into cells in your brain. Later when you want to recall it you can recall that physical memory into consciousness again.

"Suppose something like that happens when the genome 'thinks.' Like us, it will make changes to its 'brain.' But its brain consists of chromosomes and the genes along those chromosomes. And genes are what define species of living creatures! So just by thinking, the genome can write changes into genes along the chromosomes it consist of, bringing new species into existence. On this side of the revolution, people think of species as 'really' ideas stored in memory. They're ideas the genome can recall, think changes to, and store back in memory as a new species.

"What I'm supposing for the genome isn't something unreal. It's nothing more than what we humans do when we think.

"Idea Number Four is: The genome is conscious and intelligent and creative—it can think new species into existence merely by bringing to mind the idea of an existing species and thinking changes back into its genes."

Jane turns to the controls. "The first landfall's coming up." She turns back to face us. "I'll give you a few Pointers to help you feel at home.

"Even this early in the revolution, the world looks different. I'll help you see the world the way people here do. Wherever we look we're aware of not matter but life. In our homes everything we see is made of wood or leather and bone or fabrics made from plants. Outside we don't see mountains made of rock, we see forests. The ground isn't rocks and sand, we see the grass and weeds that cover it, we know the soil is rich in bacteria, insects, worms. It's teeming with life. Even the clouds we know to be mostly water vapor given up by plants, they are a sign of life too. And because we know it evolved, wherever there's life we see consciousness. Even this early in the revolution, physical matter has become remote. Our primary reality will be consciousness, in ourselves and in the world of evolved creatures all around us.

"That's a big advance over your time. For you it was consciousness that seemed remote. The only example of it you knew about was locked away in each person's conscious experience. Your scientists could draw maps of what was going on in people's brains, but they couldn't study the experience of consciousness itself. To them, consciousness was more remote than the far side of the moon.

"But once you have two examples of something, as people do now, studying it becomes much easier. Once people realized the genome was conscious they could study consciousness not only in their own conscious experiences but also in the world around them in the form of living creatures.

"So what are those consciousnesses in nature

like? Remember I said each genome opens up a consciousness in mind. Now, our consciousnesses can't communicate with one another directly, there seem to be barriers between them. But the consciousnesses set up by genomes can, they can communicate with one another in mind. The result is a genome consciousness at every level inside our bodies, from individual cells up through each organ and tissue to the individual itself. And beyond the individual there'll be a genome-consciousness for each species, each order, even each kingdom, all the way up to all of nature itself." Jane turns away to manage our landfall.

Landfall Number One: Revolution in Biology

We're coming in to make landfall at a future college campus. It's vast. What's that huge building there, right in the center? "That's the nature study complex," Jane says. So where are the physical science departments? "They're in those small buildings scattered around the edge of campus." So what are all those buildings grouped there, around the nature-study complex? "Those are departments for the humanities. When evolution involves consciousness you can study it much better through the methods of the humanities than through the methods of the physical sciences. The study of evolution has gravitated back from the sciences to the humanities."

We come in for landfall right next to the nature study complex. Jane leads us inside to take a look.

Inside it's nothing but a maze of corridors, each one lined with small rooms along both sides.

What are people in these rooms doing? "They're compiling biographies, one for each node in each level of the genome-intelligences," Jane says. "Each genome-intelligence has its own personality and capabilities. Some drove the evolution of their species furiously for tens of millions of years then seemed to lose interest and let all their creatures go extinct, as happened to trilobites. Others fashioned creatures of an entirely new kind, like sharks, and then doggedly preserved them almost unchanged for hundreds of millions of years. The true story of evolution, it turns out, is better told in terms of the evolution of genomes, in mind, rather than of their creatures in the physical world."

First step in our trip—biology has been revolutionized.

Back in the time machine Jane gets us under way. "We're traveling on post-revolutionary ideas now," she says.

"Idea Number Five: Evolution is creative.

"Once people accepted the process of evolution was conscious, they accepted it also had free will, it could be creative," she says. "Non-living matter doesn't have free will—a volcano can't decide whether to erupt—and non-living matter can't be creative— snowflakes still come in the same hundred or so patterns they always have. Consciousness, free will and creativity, on the other hand, all involve non-physical processes special to mind.

"And if the process of evolution was conscious, creative, and had free will, that must be where we got our consciousness, creativity and free will from. Genomes evolved before we did!"

That's going to be the focus of our next landfall. "Idea Number Five: Evolution is the source of all creativity on Earth."

Landfall Number Two: Revolutions in Philosophy and Physics

For our second landfall we glide silently through walls and corridors, ending up settling gently in what looks like a laboratory. It's filled with chairs and desks but all around us are posted graphs telling us that something like experimental science has re-appeared.

Here's what Jane tells us: The new science is made possible by the invention of a new unit of measurement, the creatron. That's how much know-how an orb spider comes into the world with. It knows it can drop itself down on a line of silk but must climb back up to return—it knows about gravity. To lay out its web in a flat plane it has to pick its way through the world to the various anchor points; it has to know about space in three dimensions. To spin its web it must know about the production and deployment of five different kinds of silk.

With that unit established, you could measure the creativity of genomes throughout every level of nature—species, orders, entire kingdoms, even all of nature. At each higher level the creatron scores soared. The creativity of all of nature was so enormous you couldn't distinguish it from complete freedom from determinism by physics. The old philosophical debate about determinism versus free will was finally laid to rest. Evolved creatures, like us, sharing in all of nature's freedom from determinism, could be creative, we could have free will too. Unlike purely physical things we weren't bound by the laws of physics, by prior chains of physical events. We could choose to go along with them or strike out on our own.

Those laws of physics? The more creativity people found in nature the less they found to apply those laws to, until it didn't seem to matter whether those laws applied at all.

Now physics had been made over by the revolution in evolution.

Back into the time machine. "End of the line coming up," says Jane. "Eventually, worlds reached through time travel would become too strange for you to make any sense of. Our last landfall will be just short of that point. Since your understanding will be as limited as that of a child there, we make landfall in a school classroom.

"Just bear this in mind—everything you've learned so far has melted down to become part of the mother tongue these people learn as infants. I have to introduce you to just one more idea before we land.

Idea Number Six: Thinking equals evolving

"The genome 'evolves' new kinds of creatures by thinking them into existence. So for the genome, evolving involves thinking. Could that be true for us, too? How about our thinking? Could thinking in us involve something evolving? Could thinking be our thoughts evolving, each one out of the one before, in mind? It could, if we want it to, we've no reason or logic for denying it. How simple that makes everything! Anything which isn't physical, is something evolving. No more mysteries. So idea Number Six is, thinking equals evolving, both take place through non-physical processes operating in mind."

We make landfall in a classroom.

Landfall Number Three: Revolution in Human Nature

"What makes us humans different from all other living creatures is how we think," our teacher tells us, "We think by creating thoughts and letting them evolve. What you need to learn now is the various ways living creatures evolve, so your thoughts can evolve like that, too."

Back in Landfall One, early in the revolution, we saw the genome intelligences being identified. In Landfall Two we saw them being assessed for their creative intelligence. Once they had had their creativity assessed, some stood out as exceptional. Surely, people thought, these genomes must have invented new "engines" to speed evolution up and make it more efficient. Patiently human engineers of the time teased apart the non-physical processes those engines consisted of, until out of those engines they had created an entirely new set of mental tools that gave human thinking access to the creative power of evolution itself.

These are the tools children are being taught in class today. They are the final fruits, as far as we can follow them, of a revolution set in motion centuries ago, when we first asked ourselves what it meant we evolved.

We can understand nothing they are being told. We reboard our vehicle.

"No more, Jane? Can't you tell us a little more?"

"I can tell you in outline. In your day you'd already taken a big step; in just a century you'd already begun removing yourself from competition with other living species, doubling your life expectancy. Instead you'd begun putting your thoughts in your place, to evolve for you. Now, by adopting the genome's tools, humans are on track to elevate their own intelligence to genome-intelligence levels. Humans will then be able to direct their own evolution. Human nature will become both technology and the ultimate art.

"Already people like the teacher in that classroom look back to the evolution revolution in your time as the crucial hinge in history."

That's as far as Jane can take us. She scoots us back to our own time. Say goodbye to Jane. "Goodbye Jane."

Spoiler

For readers who go straight to a book's "Conclusion" to see if it's likely to interest them, I've provided this spoiler.

Within, a rigorous re-formulation of "folk psychology" capable of supplanting—and preferable to—physical determinism in today's natural philosophy. Central idea: Evolution is managed by an agent, the process of evolution itself. This agent comes embodied in genomes—first genomes evolved into existence, then they evolved further to become able to create living creatures like us. They made us conscious and creative by embedding in us mental talents corresponding to their own.

I didn't discover this. It's not meant to be science. It's offered as a heuristic device, a thinking tool. It starts with saying, what matters most to us is what we're like, conscious and creative, and what's most responsible for that is us having evolved. By giving the agent responsible for making us mental talents corresponding to ours, to our consciousness and creativity, talents that clearly are not physical, and by giving the process of evolution its own nature and its own rules, I distinguish that process from physics, while making them both, physics and evolution, equally "real."

Doing so provides support for folk psychology, the common-sense belief that our nature has roots in both physical matter/force and consciousness plus free will.

From this basic idea come two other basic ideas. The first reshapes the world around us. It says, with evolution a source of wisdom entered the world, manifested as genomes, that can work on physical matter creatively and wisely, to fashion living creatures violating physical determinism. The second idea reshapes human nature. It says, there's a source of wisdom in the world that made us as wise as we are and that, through the study of it, we could make ourselves wiser still.

From these two ideas come others: a new origin of species; thinking accounted for as our thoughts evolving; consciousness accounted for as a consequence of our thoughts evolving. All of these ideas concern what science has the most difficulty explaining.

We went through a similar change in world view a few centuries ago when Galileo, Francis Bacon, Descartes and Newton came up with the natural philosophy we subscribe to today. But partly as a result we've ended up with a view of ourselves that we're not all entirely happy with. Today we might prefer something different.

I'm not claiming this magical world view is new. It's similar to how the Ancient Stoics saw the world and themselves. Stoicism ultimately couldn't satisfy all people's needs and they opted instead for the consolations of Christianity. But the discovery we evolved could provide Stoicism with a rationale it previously lacked. Updating Stoicism for our own time, substituting the genome for their World Spirit, may provide us with an opportunity to rejoin and continue the classical philosophical tradition.

> "And, finally, when we have surveyed the process of evolution, we shall have to ask what judgment we can make about it. Is it good or bad, beautiful or ugly, directed or undirected? These are largely value-judgments, and are thus not scientific. But it is the answer to them which makes evolution interesting to the ordinary educated man and woman."
>
> *J B S Haldane, "The Causes of Evolution," 1932.*

Readings

The Origin of Consciousness in the Breakdown of the Bicameral Mind, by Julian Jaynes. This book is fundamental to how I think about consciousness. Jaynes plots how consciousness like ours arose from 3000 to 500 BC.

Zoonomia, by Erasmus Darwin, published 1794. How thinking about evolution started. Picking up from where Aristotle left off and adding to it discoveries made using microscopes, Erasmus lays the foundations for almost all our present-day ideas about evolution, and probably a great deal more if we're receptive.

The Body: A Guide for Occupants, by Bill Bryson, published in 2019. A hugely entertaining account of how wonderful the human body is.

The Complete Human Body: The Definitive Visual Guide, by Alice Roberts, also published 2019. A superb richly graphic companion to Bryson's book.

Reviews of "Classic Evolutionary texts" published at evolutionforthehumanities.com/book-reviews.

For a cosmology along the lines of the magic in this book, podcast, "The Chuck Darwin Show," https://evolvedself.podbean.com, top (latest) item.

Made in USA - Kendallville, IN
1208976_9780977947096
02.15.2021 1827